ARTIST IN CHRYSALIS

A Biographical Study of Goethe in Italy

University of Illinois Press

Urbana   Chicago   London

Artist in Chrysalis

A BIOGRAPHICAL STUDY OF GOETHE IN ITALY

H. G. HAILE

Preface

N O MAN has left us with a more
thoughtful and honest account of his own development or a better general treatment of the intellectual climates in which it occurred than Goethe did. Here may lie the principal reason for
the dearth of true biographies in the extensive literature about
him. Scholars, understandably preoccupied with his poetic accomplishments, have as a rule recognized that these form a pe-
culiarly suitable introduction to the man. Anyone exclusively
interested in his life can do no better than to turn to Goethe's
own nine volumes of strictly autobiographical writing, while his
immense correspondence and diaries invite us to a lifetime's study
in the most poetic materials of this sort ever written.

With men whose primary importance is in statesmanship, let
us say, or science, the goal of a biographer may well be to evalu-
ate their accomplishments in the context of their lives. It was
at one time expected that the biographer of a poet would also
treat the man's works. In our era, criticism has argued that the
relationship between the artist and his art is quite irrelevant to
appreciation of an artwork. If this is true, then biography is out
of bounds for the study of poetry, and there remains no other
orientation for the biography of a poet than the life itself. Focus
on the man would seem all the more appropriate with a foreign
poet, whose works are probably remote from the biographer's

audience. My hope in writing about Goethe is to offer a brief and straightforward introduction and invitation to a fascinating personality.

It goes without saying that his deeds are crucial to our understanding of his personality; I could not avoid relying heavily on Goethe's poetic works. The book is organized in accordance with them, most of its chapters taking individual major works as their theme. For that reason I am eager to emphasize that my aim is not a commentary on Goethe's writing. My view of his personality may have implications for the interpretation of his poetry, but I do not enter into the history of Goethe criticism or take explicit issue with it. I am proceeding on an assumption, widespread among Goethe students, that while he was tremendously versatile and productive in many fields, including literature, his true greatness was as a human being.

Posterity imposes penalties on the great man. It invariably places his image in the service of its passing cultural and moral purposes and seeks to eternalize him as a magnificent paragon. Within a short time the man fades behind his own imposing monument. It stands there as an object of indifference for most of humanity. Some few may mock its incredible pompousness, but convention upholds it as a cultural fixture important for the status quo. Goethe studies offer perhaps the best example of this sort of adulation, and most biographers have sentimentally accepted it or, perhaps worse, reacted all too coldly and cynically against it. A major hope of any writer on Goethe is to get at the genuine man with the help of and despite the mass of literature about him.

Yet all biography confronts the fundamental dilemma imposed by our own human intellectual limitations. While all our surroundings are in constant flow from one form into another like clouds in the sky, our techniques are seldom adapted to continuity: we try to replicate our world in all kinds of still shots.

Goethe's being transcended the moment, but we are constrained to capture it by showing successive stages in his carer. An orderly and sequential description of events, although easy to arrange and deceptively easy to read, does not yield a very true impression of life. What we are accustomed to perceiving in the world about us is flux, and a book is unable to reproduce that. It follows that biographer and reader alike must try to engage their fancy in such a way as to produce a living moment analogous to their perception of natural stimuli; i.e., challenging the imagination is the main task of biography.

I offer in the pages to come just a glimpse of the man Goethe, a snapshot which may be more interesting than some others in that it is somewhat enigmatic: his trip to Italy at the age of thirty-seven. His main purpose there was revision of his collected works for their first publication as such. All of them had been of an expressive, even confessional sort. Together they seemed to him to be a summary of his true self. His work in Rome brought most of the important stretches of his life to the fore again. He had to seek understanding for past actions and attitudes alien to him now. The attempt was not easy or by any means always successful, but sympathetic examination of his past meant a quiet kind of growth and, eventually, a more perfect present. Goethe went to Italy as a man of many parts, often unproductive and frustrated because of the diverse demands placed on *and by* his varied talents. He returned from Italy as a self-confessed artist. However problematic this new identity proved to be in subsequent years, it was Goethe's first integrated vision of his own personality.

The process of integration is what I want to show. My purpose is not to provide the detailed inventory of a career. My reader may not even feel that he is being given a very conscientious account of the stay in Italy. I do hope that a poet in his late thirties can gradually take on dimension and color in the fancy, and that it may be possible at last to feel reasonably well acquainted with him at one specific time in his development: that crucial period when his commitment to an artist's life became final.

The University of Illinois Research Board and the University of Illinois Center for Advanced Study generously supported work which went into this volume.

Contents

ABBREVIATIONS

Translations from the German are my own. In the case of Goethe's letters and diaries, they are based on *Goethes Werke, III.-IV. Abtheilung* (Weimar, 1887-1919). I refer to the autobiography *Dichtung und Wahrheit* by section, or *Buch,* and to the *Italienische Reise* by date. In the case of other poetic works I cite where possible the popular edition widely available in American libraries, the so-called *Jubiläums-Ausgabe.* I have used the following abbreviations.

Bode   Wilhelm Bode. *Goethe in vertraulichen Briefen seiner Zeitgenossen.* Vol. I. Berlin, 1921.

DjG   Hanna Fischer-Lamberg. *Der junge Goethe.* Vols. I-IV. Berlin, 1963–.

Grumach   Ernst and Renate Grumach. *Goethe: Begegnungen und Gespräche.* Vols. I and II. Berlin, 1965–.

Herwig   Wolfgang Herwig. *Goethes Gespräche.* Vol. I. Zurich, 1965.

JA   *Goethes Werke.* 40 vols. Stuttgart and Tübingen, 1902–1912.

LA   *Goethe: Die Schriften zur Naturwissenschaft.* Vols. I-X. Weimar, 1947–.

Hegira

A STUDENT capable of trans-
porting himself back into the year 1786 might be able to develop
some idea of the condition in which I had then been captive for
ten years, but it would be a challenge even for a psychologist,
because to reproduce it would require attention to all my duties,
desires, obligations, and diversions" — thus the old Goethe[1] reflects about the years in which he had turned his energies to the
welfare of the little Saxon duchy Weimar. To outward appear-
ances he had been the brilliant President of the Chamber, his
efforts obvious in such diverse sectors as road improvement in
outlying districts and light operettas for the lords and ladies at
court. The psychological undercurrents to which he refers were
not suspected even by close friends until the time of his well-
prepared but abrupt disappearance from Weimar in September,
1786.

In November he reported himself in Rome, and he did not
return from there for almost two years. His old friends then found
him a different man, middle-aged, a bit inclined toward corpu-
lence, expressly determined no longer to devote his life to the
welfare of others, but to seek an ideal development of his own
personality with particular attention to aesthetic pursuits. The
sojourn in Italy marked a kind of perihelion in his career. Closer
to the sun, a last strong creative urge brought frustrated artistic

plans of a dozen and more years to fruition. After Italy there followed an awkward vacuum, a groping for new beginnings and an adjustment to a less inspired life tempo.

Various silhouettes picture Goethe before Italy as a slender and elegant gentleman. Portraits show an eloquent mouth, high arched nose, and the graceful bearing which bespoke the rococo ideal of the *ancien régime*. Whoever met him remembered large, urgent eyes, and many noted a certain tension, as, for example, did a young lady in 1783: "His physiognomy shows intelligence, heavy bones over his eyes and very thin lips. The eyes are serious and large. A kind of stiffness in the way he moves his head gives him an unattractive air, but he is a fine man who has my complete favor. He is on very good terms with the other Privy Councilors, all of whom must defer to him even though he is the youngest and most recently ennobled."[2] About eighteen months later another girl entered in her diary: "There is something horribly stiff about his whole manner, and he speaks very little. I always supposed it was his greatness that made him ill at ease. However that may be, everyone who knows him intimately says that he is conscientious and honest in office and that he secretly helps poor people. But the same ones say that his new position [Acting President of the Chamber] has brought an alien trait to his character which some call pride, others weakness."[3]

In actuality, he had long since accustomed himself to "greatness." He had become very famous in Germany during his early twenties with the highly unconventional play *Götz von Berlichingen*. It was followed by a short tragic novel, *The Sorrows of Young Werther*, which swept Europe and made an international celebrity of the young author in that era when ladies' hearts beat to the vicissitudes of their favorite poet's love life, and the tears of the educated man flowed tenderly for eloquent writing. Before he was twenty-five Goethe had become the central figure of a generation in reaction against the Rococo Enlightenment. The

2

young were railing against social and political institutions in a frank new way and in a strong new language for which he had, in large measure, set the tone. Caught up in the vogue, the eighteen-year-old Duke of Weimar had invited him to his residence in the fall of 1775, and he installed him in office the following summer. From that time on, Goethe did all he could to dissociate himself from the so-called storm and stress generation without alienating his youthful lord, who continued to elevate him in rank and authority.

Since he had published nothing more of consequence, he was frequently not even thought of as an author anymore, so that the two young ladies just quoted tended to look upon him as a busy and powerful political figure. Ultimate authority in the little realm (population 100,000, area 730 square miles) lay with Duke Carl August, for this was still the day of absolutism — or, more accurately by the last quarter of the century, of benevolent paternalism. Still, the ruler of such a tiny principality was sorely restricted by finance and very dependent on the judicious calculations of his ministerial staff. Even as a rash youth, Carl August usually deferred to the advice of his governmental commissions — although Goethe's appointment and rapid rise illustrate how effective the sovereign's will could be in individual instances. By and large Goethe had proved to be a good and independent minister, something possible only for an official who enjoyed princely friendship and admiration.

We must not imagine that official life in a rural duchy was normally as demanding as even the quieter reaches of a modern bureaucracy, where an officeholder is in any case expected to devote the better part of his day to the job. Only the copyists in Chancellery were likely to spend as many as eight hours at their tedious work. Although he had entered into more obligations than anyone else, Goethe was still able to insist that "science and letters" constituted his true calling.[4] The writer who lived from some ministerial post or other presented a frequent phenomenon at the courts in Germany. The land's most brilliant and prolific novelist, Christoph Martin Wieland, was not able to speak of writing as his ostensible living until his late forties, although he had been devoting most of his time to it for twenty years by then. Goethe did allow official duties to consume an exceptionally large portion of his energies during his first ten years in Weimar, but he was acting more in accordance with needs inherent in his personality than in conformity with contemporary official life.

He came from middle-class Frankfurt Protestants who had attained financial and social standing by dint of hard work and thrift. The boy's mind early evolved that characteristic ethos which demanded self-denial and some worthy cause in which to invest his talents. It was in this sense that he sought political position, so he was naturally suspicious of the benefits which accrued to himself. "That a man can do so much for himself and so little for others! That our wish to help others is almost never granted! I have carried almost all my personal talents to a pinnacle of success — or at least I can see success coming. For others I work myself down and accomplish nothing" — this from the thirty-two-year-old. It is from one of his strikingly candid letters to Lady Charlotte von Stein,[5] with whom his correspondence in these Weimar years was so prolific as to keep us unusually well informed about his activities and his reflections on them. The great number of letters is partly accounted for by the many days he spent away from Weimar inspecting roads, crops, weavers' "factories," etc., looking to combat poverty now by reworking old silver mines in the mountains, now by attempting new irrigation techniques in the fields. As the years passed he came to feel that most of his energies were being consumed by mere shoring operations and emergency makeshifts. When, in 1779, the Weimar Council received a demand for troops from the importunate Frederick II of Prussia, it was Goethe who was charged with

4

weighing various alternatives, and he who at last rode from village to village levying recruits.

Weimar offered him an opportunity rare enough for a middle-class youth of his period: "It is a bold and proud wish, the wish to do good. We must be very grateful if only a small part of it is granted us,"[6] he said. Such a wish, insofar as it entailed political involvement, was one which only a hereditary ruler could grant. The same circumstance which opened Weimar to Goethe (that its duke was an enthusiastic boy who admired him) also made the territory appear well suited to his aspirations, since Carl August was intelligent and responsive to the educational efforts of the older man. The task did not turn out to be as easy as it might have seemed at first, however, and Goethe was never fully satisfied with his pupil's development. As the maturing Carl August became more strong-willed and self-assertive, he did not become less impulsive or prone to foolish peccadillos: "The duke's vision is, at basis, very limited," Goethe admitted, "so that his bold enterprises are only hare-brained larks, because he lacks judgment and true resolve."[7]

A serious parting of ways came on the issue of Weimar's role in European politics. Tension between the great powers Austria and Prussia often worked to the disadvantage of the many tiny principalities. Weimar's granting troops to Frederick, for example, clearly gave Austria a pretext for impressing a Weimar contingent, too. There were those who felt that an alliance among the smaller German states would provide a desirable balance. The Union of Princes, which thus began to be negotiated in 1783, meant for Carl August the welcome prospect of a more assertive posture, but Goethe could see in it only an expensive and undignified entanglement. Unlike Carl August, he favored a negligible international role for Weimar and hoped that its young ruler would at last grow to the same paternal affection for the land and lives that motivated Goethe himself. Ironically,

Carl August's complete confidence in his friend led him to involve Goethe, as his private secretary, in secret negotiations on behalf of the Union while he himself played the unseemly part of incognito diplomatic courier from one court to another. It was perhaps with this sort of chore in mind that Goethe dated a letter "At Ixion's Wheel, 20 February 1785." In this month his hitherto regular attendance at Privy Council sessions ceased. March through August he was present at only two of forty-three meetings.

During the spring Frederick himself took an interest in the Union of Princes, and the two-year-old scheme became reality in a matter of months. As alignment with one of the great powers, the Union took on a better color in Goethe's eyes. He could not, in any event, avoid participation in the agreements concluding Weimar's entrance, and he attended six Council sessions in the month of September, 1785, but he did not return. He probably best expressed his feelings on the subject in a later remark to Charlotte von Stein: "It is my firm opinion that anyone who gets involved in administration and is not himself the ruling lord is either a Philistine or a knave or a fool."[8]

The nature of a minister's position at the eighteenth-century court was obviously such that the public trust, however sacred he himself held it to be, might be taken lightly by the hereditary prince who had appointed him. Goethe had to learn this by bitter experience:

> I am no longer in the least surprised that most hereditary rulers are so crazy, stupid and silly. Very few have such a promising natural potential as our duke, seldom is a ruler surrounded by so many intelligent, good men who are his friends — but still no proper start can be made, the tadpole with its fishtail is back before you know it. . . . With all his passion for what is good and right, he does not find it as natural as he does what is unseemly. It is wonderful how intelligent he can be, his insight, his knowl-

edge, and yet to enjoy himself he has to do something silly. . . . I am sorry to say that it is in his nature, that although the frog can exist on dry land for a time, he is made for the water.[9]

At this writing Goethe happened to be exasperated by Carl August's persistent importation of wild hogs which rooted up his impoverished subjects' crops and tore apart their hedges all year long only to permit the feudal pleasure of the chase in winter, itself a highly destructive and dangerous affair. Goethe's ability to put up with this sort of irritation, to swallow his pride when his most urgent entreaties were — as on this subject — ignored, and to continue his efforts in behalf of Weimar, probably contributed more than any other single factor to the gradually improved quality of the administration and the slow education of Carl August as one of Europe's more enlightened rulers in the first quarter of the nineteenth century. Yet the same tenacity which Goethe demonstrated before 1785 makes his sudden flight in 1786 seem all the more improbable. How can he have been willing to sacrifice position and personal advantage together with the ideals for which he had given his best years, and what did he hope to gain?

He himself tended to regard the circumstances surrounding the departure for Italy as mysterious, so we have little hope of clarifying them today. Nevertheless, we can observe how, in the middle 1780's, certain factors seem to have converged which, in retrospect, appear connected with his trip. The slow accretion of frustrations in office, a growing dissatisfaction with the nobility and the feudal system, his own flagging health, a slight staleness in his famous friendship with the Lady von Stein, and a life-long wish to visit Italy were important background factors. The events which may have precipitated the final decision seem to have occurred about a year before it was actually carried through, or during the late summer of 1785. That fall he probably determined his destination and began making the arrangements in Weimar and in Venice and Rome which would permit the startlingly abrupt departure in September, 1786.

Goethe made his first visit to the highly fashionable international spa at Carlsbad in July, 1785. It did wonders for his health, and he enjoyed himself immensely. This was his first prolonged contact with the highest European nobility — from Russia, France, and Austria, as well as from Germany — and they were charming. The lords and ladies were delighted to meet the author of *Werther* and, since he had been ennobled in 1782, to associate with him. Especially the ladies feted him and were generous with favors of a sort which a minister perhaps could not accept, but which were nevertheless flattering. He left Carlsbad on August 16, spending a week inspecting Bohemian mining regions and visiting friends before heading back to Saxony. Before he arrived he was met by the news of the Necklace Affair in Paris. It rose up before him "like a Gorgon's head,"[10] jolting him back to reality.

The Cardinal of France had been arrested. On behalf of the Queen of France, so went the first report, he had contracted for a diamond necklace which was worth twenty million livres. The notorious spiritualist di Cagliostro was somehow involved. The necklace had disappeared and been broken up, and the stones had been disposed of in Holland and England. What Goethe had known all along about Europe's lighthearted ruling set seemed confirmed. To one so familiar with the bankrupt economies which supported such frivolities as theirs, the consequences seemed disastrous.

A few months were to pass before full details reached Weimar. Di Cagliostro turned out to be only peripherally involved. Marie Antoinette probably knew nothing of the swindle itself, although members of the French nobility who enjoyed her confidence had clearly used their positions to hoodwink Cardinal Rohan. His role had indeed been a shameful one. Thus Goethe's first impression seemed substantially borne out: "In the immoral abyss of city, court and state which opened up here before me I thought I could perceive, ghostlike, the most hideous consequences, and I could not free myself of the vision for a long time. I behaved so strangely that some friends whom I was visiting in the country when first news came of the scandal thought I had gone out of my mind."[11] The Necklace Affair struck Goethe so strongly as an omen of the coming upheaval because it confirmed traits which he had long recognized in Europe's ruling families — with whom he had just spent several delightful, carefree weeks. Incidentally, there can be no doubt that he did prophetically connect the scandal with the French Revolution. Already in 1781, in taking note of the same scoundrel, di Cagliostro, he had made the really very frightening remark: "Believe me, our moral and political world is tunneled through with subterranean passageways, cellars and sewers like a metropolis. Almost no one takes thought of their intercrossings and of their denizens, but whoever does know something of them finds it much more comprehensible when suddenly the ground caves in somewhere, or smoke rises up from a crevasse, or someplace else wondrous voices are heard."[12] To the man who wrote such lines, the Necklace Affair revealed nothing altogether unsuspected about European court life, but for that very reason it must have been terribly shocking to one who had attached his entire career to the nobility's good will and good character.

Goethe had a number of letters to write when he returned from Carlsbad to Weimar at the end of August, 1785, so we can draw from them a fair record of what was occupying his mind. One of his first acts was to send for the four-volume set of his collected works — an unauthorized edition, for he had never undertaken one himself. Nor did he have the leisure to do so now, but in Carlsbad he had been reminded that the world still thought of him as an author. Another of his letters contains instructions for the burial of Kraft, a cashiered, psychotic civil servant who had been totally dependent on him for several years. A farewell note to the Lady Charlotte as she departs for her country residence reveals another of their petty spats. His birthday on August 28, often a pleasant little occasion for the two of them, finds him this year in stiff court regalia on the palace steps to receive the Prussian emissary, just arrived to discuss Weimar's entry into the Union of Princes. On the day after the diplomat's departure, Goethe again finds time to write some personal letters: "Nothing has changed here — and that is really a shame, for it might have been a beautiful structure, high and expansive, but it has, unfortunately, no foundation. What does have a foundation on the unsteady earth?"[13] His reference pretty clearly is to Saxe-Weimar, but the same metaphor of a structure wanting adequate foundation was becoming a favorite one for describing his own life. After the negotiations have been concluded, he writes scornfully: "The duke is happy in his pack, and that is just fine with me. The courtiers are dispatched, the hounds called in, and it is all the same, a lot of noise to chase a hare to death."[14] Our next surviving letter is dated: "8 September, 3:30 A.M." A diplomatic courier has arrived in the middle of the night and Goethe, unable to go back to sleep, reports taking up "Necker's new work." It may be mere coincidence that he mentions the three volumes *De l'Administration des finances de la France* for the first time in these heavy September days — they had been published the year before — but as it turned out this reading may have constituted an event of importance second only to the Necklace Affair in prompting a decision to escape from Weimar.

Jacques Necker was the gifted Swiss economist who, although known to literature perhaps as the father of Madame de Staël, asserted an important place in history by serving France well as director of the treasury from 1776 to 1781. Goethe had received

Necker's earlier book, the famous *Compte rendu au roi* (1781), at a time when he was deeply concerned about Weimar's disastrous finances. He read it immediately, bored his friends by talking of nothing else, and referred to it as a "tremendous heritage for the world and for posterity."[15] Since it was the first publication of a national budget on the continent, his enthusiasm was not exaggerated.

He was conscious of certain parallels between his own career and Necker's. Both took office in 1776, Goethe eventually assuming the direct counterpart of Necker's ministry. Like him, he was not accorded the title that went with the important post. In Necker's case insufficient authority, together with Marie Antoinette's capriciousness, led to his resignation in the very year that he published *Compte rendu*. The Necklace Affair certainly seemed to vindicate Necker now. The effect of his latest work, *De l'Administration des finances,* on the acting president of the Weimar Chamber must have been discouraging. The sound procedures described here contrasted with the confused state of French finances since Necker's resignation — as the author intended they should — but they also contrasted with Goethe's own shabby experiences in the Weimar economy. No doubt he was most intrigued by the question raised on the very first pages as to just when a high public official can in good conscience resign his office of trust. Necker disdains those who "choose the moment of their resignation in which they may enjoy the embarrassment of a successor." The "great concerns of state," he argues, "must take priority over such seducing calculations of self love," and he concludes that "only when a man is no longer essentially necessary is it perhaps justifiable if he permit himself to think of himself."[16]

Goethe seems immediately to have set about making himself no longer essentially necessary. In November he was able to write of certain sectors: "What I have begun here is going well and will improve from year to year. If I can just hold out, endure a little longer, then I will be to the point where things will take care of themselves for a while."[17] He did not leave Weimar until he felt he could in good conscience write to Carl August: "The affairs of your house are in good order and making progress. I know that you will permit me now to think of myself — you have often enough urged me to do so. In general, I know that I can be dispensed with at the present moment. As concerns the affairs assigned to me, I have left them in an order which will proceed well without me for a time. I could fall dead and my office would suffer no interruption."[18] To write these words on the eve of departure in 1786 had required long and careful planning in official matters. We can only guess about his arrangements for a dwelling in Rome and for the transfer of funds through a Leipzig business house, because Goethe hated to discuss important projects until he felt them practically accomplished. We have no reference to his plans until a remark at the end of December, 1785, that he does not know what the new year will bring: "I do not care to contemplate large, expansive prospects."[19]

The great attraction which Italy exerted on Goethe can be compared only with the fascination which it has held for his biographers, who have turned his lifetime's "longing" for Italy into one of the best-known *topoi* of world literature. It was certainly appropriate for them to do so. The fashionable eighteenth century early accepted an Italian voyage as the final touch for true cultivation. Goethe's father had recorded his own *viaggio* in a journal composed in Italian; he hired a native speaker to edit the work and later to teach his children the language. By the time Wolfgang was grown, he was accustomed to informing even strangers that he planned his Italian trip for the near future. One who knew the twenty-four-year-old only as *Herr Göde* reported: "He sketches and paints, too. His room is filled with nice prints of the best ancient masters. . . . He intends to go to Italy to inform himself properly."[20] Old Bodmer (the literary critic in Switzerland) knew from gossip *before* Goethe paid him a visit: "He is only twenty-five or twenty-six years old. He plans to travel in Italy."[21] Against this background the touching declaration of Goethe in Venice seems understandable:

> I thank God that I have learned to treasure again the things dear to me from my boyhood. How happy I am that I can approach the classics again. I can say it now, I can confess my pathological foolishness now. During the past few years I have not been able to look at a Latin author or to think about anything which evoked an image of Italy. When I came upon such things by chance I suffered the most terrible pain. . . . If I had not made this decision which I am now carrying through I would have perished. The desire to see these objects with my own eyes, to let them rise up in my own soul, had become overripe. My historical studies had been blocked, because an impenetrable wall was separating me from material at my very fingertips. Even now I do not feel as if I were seeing Italy for the first time, but as if I were returning.[22]

A boyhood friend, the composer Philipp Kayser, went to Italy in 1784, long before Goethe began to entertain realistic plans. He wrote to Kayser that he envied his having "entered into the land which I, like a sinful prophet, still see lying out before me in the distance."[23] When the two collaborated on an operetta, Goethe complained bitterly: "I pity my poor operetta the way one might pity a child to be born of a Negro woman into slavery. . . . I just pity poor Kayser that he has to waste his music on this barbaric [German] language."[24] Such hard words came only in early 1786, after he had seen his way clear to perfecting his Italian at the source. Soon he even risked a daring allusion in a letter to Kayser, and was himself carried away by his metaphor: "If I had just mastered the Italian language as well as I have my unhappy German, I would not hesitate to invite you to a journey beyond the Alps, and we would surely make our fortunes there. Fare you well you sole survivor from my youth, matured so quietly that I can scarce believe it. Fare you well."[25]

We have no way of knowing when Goethe's actual decision occurred, but an interesting excursion into dream psychology encourages us to accept October, 1785, as a time when he must have been giving serious thought to it. From his early weeks in Rome we have repeated references to a dream. It had made a very strong impression on him; he had discussed it with his friends in Weimar at the time and does not need to remind them of the details now: "Remember the pheasant dream? It is now being fulfilled. I hope that the ending will be better."[26] He assures them that he is enjoying Rome on their behalf "and preparing a magnificent feast of pheasants for you."[27] He tells Charlotte: "Laden with pheasants I am thinking only of returning and bringing the best to you."[28] We find an equally enigmatic note made in his diary when passing through Bologna: "The pheasant dream is beginning to be fulfilled, for truly the cargo I am taking on can be compared with that precious fowl, and I sense the outcome, too."[29] No surviving contemporary account tells us more.

Thirty years later he published his travel diary as the *Italian Journey*. Here we have the above entry expanded as follows:

> Bologna, 19 October 1786, evening. Made anxious now by the onrush of overfulfillment in good and desirable things, I must remind my friends of a dream which seemed so significant just about one year ago. I dreamed I was landing in a pretty big boat on a fertile, heavily overgrown island where I knew the most beautiful pheasants could be had. And I did bargain for some of these fowls from the natives, who immediately produced them slaughtered in great quantity. I suppose they were pheasants, but, as dreams tend to transform everything, what appeared were long tails with colorful eyes, as of peacocks or birds of paradise. They brought heaps of them to my ship and laid them with the heads inwards, piled neatly so that the colorful

tails hanging out in the sunshine looked like the grandest hay-mows, so full that there remained but little space in front and in back for the steersman and oarsmen. Thus we cut through the calm sea while I enumerated the friends with whom I would share these colorful treasures. When we landed at last in a great harbor I clambered from deck to deck seeking a landing place for my little boat, and got lost among the tremendous masts of the ships. We take pleasure in visions like these which, since they arise from within us, must in some way be analogous with the rest of our life and destiny.

Without commenting on his ability to remember all these details, or questioning their accuracy, we must in any case accept the fact that Goethe did have a dream about pheasants in October, 1785. It was vivid enough that he told his friends about it at the time. It came to his mind again about a year later when he got to Bologna, because the dream had been connected with a future voyage, with exotic and beautiful treasures, and with an uncertain return.

Goethe was an extremely communicative person, but he was also secretive, so that talking about his dream was his only way of expressing the sense of anticipation about a great change planned in his life. Even on the eve of departure his friends appear to have been told nothing more specific than that he would not return directly from Carlsbad to Weimar. It is especially revealing of his gentle relationship with the Lady Charlotte, whom he accompanied on the first leg of her trip home from Carlsbad, that she was neither told nor did she require to know where his projected journey would take him. Carl August also appears particularly generous in granting indefinite leave without being informed as to where it would be spent or even how long it was to last. Goethe's first letters from Italy continue to be secretive — to Carl August: "Another well-wishing, happy word from afar, without place or date. Soon I shall be permitted to open my mouth and tell you how well I am faring. . . . I cannot explain how wondrous the memory of our hours together in Carlsbad seems to me now, how in your presence I felt compelled to give account, so to speak, of a large part of my past life and all the things connected with it, and how my Hegira began on your birthday. All this gives rise to the most curious visions in a superstitious person like me. What God has joined together, let no man put asunder."[30] Only in instructions written late in the evening of September 2, 1786, to his secretary Seidel (an alter ego who walked like him, looked like him, and learned to imitate his handwriting) was the eventual destination betrayed, as well as the assumed name under which he had chosen to travel: "All things considered, I can give you no earlier address than Rome: Mr. Jean Philippe Möller, c/o Mr. Joseph Cioja, Rome. You should not write to me there until you have heard from me again, unless there is some emergency. Put this letter in safekeeping and, for the rest, deny all to all. From my own mouth *no one* has had a single word."

On the following morning, he began keeping a diary: "3 September, 3:00 A.M. I slipped out of Carlsbad, I wouldn't have got away otherwise. My eagerness to leave had not escaped notice. The Countess Lanthieri played an overwhelming trump card, but I did not heed it. For it was time. I had wanted to leave on the twenty-eighth" (his birthday). The coach paused for two hours at noon — "Eger has the same elevation as Frankfurt, I enjoyed eating my noon meal near the fiftieth parallel" — but there was no other rest — "now that the chausée is good and the road downhill, our speed is unbelievable" — until Regensburg the next morning at ten. "I brought only a bag and a knapsack from Carlsbad, more than enough for my clothes, but my books and papers were cumbersome, so now I have bought me a little trunk that I really like. I have to see to it that I get away from here. A clerk at the Montag Book store — he used to be with

Hofmann in Weimar — recognized me. An author can expect
nothing good from book dealers. I denied, right to his face and
with the greatest composure, that it was I."[31] By half past noon
he was back in his coach to ride all night, all day, and all night
again to Munich. He arrived at dawn, strolled about during the
day, and spent the night there. "I am at the inn where Knebel
stays but do not want to ask about him lest I arouse uncertainty
— or dispel it."[32] His coach departed at 5:00 A.M. on the seventh;
there was an overnight stop at Mittenwald, departure at 6:00
A.M. on the eighth. That evening he was at last able to write:
"Arrived at the Brenner Pass, compelled hither, a resting place
as fine as one might wish."

While still north of the Alps Goethe confessed that he "ate a
pear publicly, just like any schoolboy."[33] Once across them he
declared: "I just eat figs the whole day long. You can imagine
that the pears have to be good here, where even lemons grow."[34]
For one who had become accustomed to the stuffy, sheltered life
of a courtier, this excursion obviously came as a stimulating
change of pace. He was happy to be unencumbered by attendants
and servants:

> The thing is that I am taking interest in the world again, try-
> ing and adjusting my powers of observation, seeing just how far
> my theories and facts will take me, whether my eye is clear, true
> and sharp, how much I can grasp while passing through so fast,
> and whether the wrinkles which have set themselves in my dis-
> position can be ironed out again. The mere fact that I have to
> wait on myself, always on guard and always maintaining my
> presence of mind, has produced an entirely new elasticity of
> spirit in the last few days. I have to keep an eye on the rates of
> exchange, handle money, pay bills, jot down notes, and do my
> own writing — I who was accustomed to demands no more tax-
> ing than thinking, reconsidering, formulating commands and
> dictating them.[35]

This sense of rejuvenation brings with it a heightened attentiveness to his own competence in assessing his environment. "I walk around and around and see, exercising my eyes and my mind. I am in good health and in good humor. My observations concerning people, nationalities, state, form of government, nature, art, culture and history are going forward. Without exerting the least effort I am able to draw the sweetest pleasure from it and to do some sound thinking about it. You know how much the immediate presence of *objects* can communicate to me, and how I am capable of conversing with *objects* all day long."[36] "I am living quietly and according to a strict regimen, so that the objects round about me do not encounter an inspired soul, but must inspire my soul instead. In the latter instance the danger of error is greatly reduced."[37]

Such a tight rein reminds us of the self-discipline of the scientist. In fact, in recent years his main creative efforts had gone to comparative anatomy and geology, but for this trip he has chosen the world of art as containing the objects on which he will test and develop his own faculties: "I try to let everything come to me, and I do not permit myself to find this or that in the object. I now observe art in the same way that I have been accustomed to observing nature, and I am achieving what I have so long striven for — a more complete grasp of the best that man, too, has produced."[38] What he is calling art is, of course, art history. He is mainly interested in the Italian Renaissance, and he is studying above all else craftsmanship and the development of techniques. His approach is a scholarly one, but it aims toward sympathy with the artist and appreciation of his work from the embryo. He says he is focusing "solely on the artist's idea in his work, his scheme of execution, the nature of the work during its first moments of life. I want to reproduce this in my soul pure, and without regard to any of the effects of time, to which everything is subject, and of change."[39]

For all his strict mental discipline and caution not to contaminate the objective world with his own notions, he was nevertheless finding his old opinions confirmed. Attitudes long characteristic of him were taking on an almost dogmatic formulation: "How happy I am that I have devóted my life to truth, for now it will be easy for me to study greatness — which is no more than the acme and the epitome of truth. The revolution which I foresaw and which is now going on within me is one which has occurred in every artist when, having long and diligently been faithful to nature, he is at last permitted to glimpse vestiges of a great, ancient spirit. His soul swells up, and he feels an inner transfiguration, a freer life on a higher plane of ease and gracc."[40] With "revolution" Goethe had not yet found the right word for the experience he was undergoing, because not new, but old insights were being evoked by the works of the Italian Renaissance. This was not to be a time of discovery for him, but one of culmination. In Venice he walked out along the Lido and noticed some crabs which had adapted themselves to life on the sea wall. "How precious and glorious is anything alive, how true, how *being!*"[41] He found the same "truth" in the Greek and Roman ruins, in that their form seemed to him organic with their function. The aqueduct at Spoleto was "so natural, efficient and true. . . . Anything that does not have a genuine inner existence has no life and cannot be brought to life and cannot be great or become great."[42] Italy was providing new, rational formulations for intuitive recognitions from Goethe's youth.

The main intellectual efforts of his mature years had involved manipulation of the external world. Now he could, for the first time, utilize the objective environment in order to become better acquainted with his own inner self. He could forget the optimum management of public policy to concentrate on his own personality and its development. Art seemed to him best suited to this purpose because it constituted the greatest challenge to all his faculties. He tried to explain to the Duchess Louise of Weimar

> that nature can be observed and appreciated more comfortably and easily than art can. The most insignificant natural product contains within itself its own mode of perfection, and if I have eyes to see I can discover the inner relationships: I am assured before I start that an entire, true existence is enclosed here within this little circle. An art work, on the other hand, draws its perfection from without. Its highest rationale is an ideal in the artist's mind which he seldom fulfills, if ever. Presumably it is also subject to certain laws which, although derived from the nature of the particular art or craft, are not so easily comprehended and deciphered as are the laws of living nature. There is also a great deal of tradition affecting art works, while each work of nature is a newly pronounced word of God.[43]

The relationship between living beings and artistic creations was a lifelong concern for Goethe. His conviction that there was in every organism a kernel of inner necessity led him to important scientific accomplishments before the Italian stay was over; in his first months preoccupation with art history crowded out other concerns.

He was eager now to think of himself as an artist, and he even toyed with the notion of becoming an expatriate: "If I just had a year of practice here and a little bit of money I'd soon be at the very top."[44] Such exuberance derived in large part from the happy discovery that his writing was again flowing easily. At the Brenner Pass he had taken out the seven-year-old manuscript of his drama *Iphigenia,* which still had to undergo major revision before being published. His only difficulty in making progress with it turned out to be a wealth of new ideas clamoring for execution. By Bologna he was ready to outline a sequel to *Iphigenia.* A little further south he had the idea for an epic poem about the return of Christ (if this is not a project he had actually begun

20

fifteen years earlier). He planned a drama about wandering
Ulysses, too, for whom he felt he had gained new understanding.
His poetic conceptions were favored whenever the coach lulled
him into a dreamlike state of semi-consciousness, a mental condition which had been most productive for him during his youth.
"Since I sleep with my clothes on," he wrote, "I don't know anything nicer than to be waked up in the morning before day to
take my seat in the coach and, half asleep, half awake, to ride
into the dawn. The Muse favored me with a good idea again
today."[45]

Goethe felt that his personality was undergoing a notable
change, and he tried many a remarkable metaphor to capture the
experience. "Sometimes I am afraid that so much is pressing in
upon me, against which I am not able to protect myself, that my
existence will grow like a snowball. Sometimes I feel that my head
cannot hold it all and bear it all. Still, everything within me is
developing, and that is the only way for me to live."[46] After two
months in Rome he offered the Lady Charlotte von Stein this account: "The more I deny the person that I was, the happier I
am. I am like a construction engineer who begins to erect a tower
after having laid a poor foundation. In tearing it down he looks
forward to the more certain solidity of his structure."[47] He had
already tried to stress the intensity of the experience in biblical
language: "Outside of Rome it is not possible to imagine how
one is schooled here. One must, so to speak, be born again, and
then one looks back on one's earlier ideas as upon childhood
things."[48] It was typical of him to resort to religious metaphors at
what he felt were turning points in his career. "There is nothing
to be compared with the new life which the contemplation of a
new country affords a thoughtful person. I may still be the same
man, but I feel that I have been transformed right down to the
marrow of my bones. . . . This place is the nexus of the entire

history of the world, and I count a second birthday, a true rebirth, from the day I entered Rome."[49]

NOTES

1. *Geschichte meines botanischen Studiums. JA* 39, 310.
2. Therese Heyne to her parents on May 2, 1783. Bode, 302 f.
3. Sophie Becker, December 30, 1784. Ibid., 325 f.
4. For example, in his letter to Charlotte von Stein on June 4, 1782.
5. April 12, 1782.
6. To Kraft on July 13, 1779.
7. To Charlotte on November 12, 1781.
8. July 10, 1786.
9. To Charlotte on March 10, 1781.
10. *Campagne in Frankreich. JA* 28, 206.
11. *Tag- und Jahreshefte* for 1789. *JA* 30, 7.
12. To Lavater on June 22, 1781.
13. To Knebel on September 1, 1785.
14. To Charlotte on September 5, 1785.
15. To Charlotte on April 2, 1781.
16. *Tome I* ([Paris?] 1784), pp. v f.
17. To Charlotte on November 9, 1785.
18. September 2, 1786.
19. To Knebel on December 30, 1785.
20. Schönborn to Gerstenberg on October 12, 1773. Grumach 1, 238 f.
21. Bodmer to Schinz on September 4, 1774. Bode, 70.
22. *Italienische Reise,* October 12, 1786.
23. June 24, 1784.
24. To Charlotte on January 26, 1786.
25. May 5, 1786.
26. To the Herders on December 13, 1786.
27. To the Herders on February 17, 1787.
28. December 29, 1786.
29. October 19, 1786.
30. Probably October 14, 1786, from Verona.
31. Diary, September 5, 1786.
32. Diary, September 5, 1786.
33. Diary, September 3, 1786.
34. *Italienische Reise,* September 12, 1786.
35. Ibid., September 11, 1786.
36. Diary, September 21, 1786.
37. Diary, September 24, 1786.

Hegira

38. To Charlotte on December 20, 1786.
39. Diary, September 25, 1786.
40. Diary, September 30, 1786.
41. *Italienische Reise,* October 9, 1786.
42. Ibid., October 27, 1786.
43. December 23, 1786.
44. Diary, October 26, 1786.
45. Diary, October 28, 1786.
46. Diary, September 27, 1786.
47. December 29, 1786.
48. To the Herders on December 19, 1786.
49. To the Herders on December 2, 1786.

Political Speculations

GOETHE was scarcely across the Alps before he began to claim that he "knew" his Italians already.[1] Like the newcomer that he was, he tended to generalize on national characteristics.[2] The word "folk" frequently occurs in his notes. From Venice, for example: "The major concept which confronts me here is the folk again. Grand mass, a necessary and natural condition." "Wherever you look it is the folk which forms the basis of everything, the entirety and not the individual."[3] His colorful descriptions of the Italians are indulgent and half-amused, but he seems confident enough of their accuracy. From Rome he even explains matter-of-factly: "My ability to discover relationships, however widely separated, and to trace them down to their origins is an extraordinary help to me."[4] He is most pleased with his observations about the nation: "I am enjoying the same success with this land as with my favorite studies. Everything depends on the first sure insight — the rest is easy."[5] But it is precisely in his other studies that he has been insisting on utmost caution and distrust of first impressions, lest he interpret his own notions into the objects.[6] We may have to make a distinction between the discipline which Goethe tried to impose on his thinking, and the native bent of his mind.

He once made a most succinct and accurate contrast between his own way of approaching a problem and that of his scientist friend, Alexander von Humboldt: "You start out with the basic components, I from the *Gestalt*."[7] To be sure, this was not until several years after Italy, at a time when Goethe, much interested in the history of science, had concluded that the major advances are attributable to radically new viewpoints which come in a flash, often independent of the researcher's volition. Some historians tend to agree with him on this score; if they are right, then science and art may be more closely related than is usually supposed. Goethe's reliance on "the first sure insight," his perception of the *Gestalt*, is especially obvious from his career as an artist. This is the way he tried to explain how he arrived at the composition of a drawing: "Here, too, I see that it is pointless for me to try to find my way out of the details into the whole; I have always had to work and develop myself from the whole into the details. Accumulation of data does not enable me to comprehend anything. I may drag up wood and straw for a long time, but I can draw no warmth from it even though there are coals underneath and smoke everywhere — then at last a gust of wind comes and flame suddenly envelops the whole thing."[8]

His analogy indicates that, while the final and all-important insight does come involuntarily, it must be prepared for by great effort. This helps explain Goethe's life-long penchant for collecting. The best-known case of long and faithfully dragging "wood and straw" was his inveterate and terrifically burdensome rock and mineral collection. He seldom made a trip without bringing back heavy boxes full, and even in Italy, when he expressly resolved to collect no rocks, he did arrive in Rome with some samples. His extensive mineral collection amounted to a mass of data which continued to smolder throughout his lifetime, occasionally flickering, but never really bursting into general flame. In other fields the very same assurance that patiently accumulated material would at last go up in a flash of understanding did bring spectacular successes. His intuitive and analogical approach to comparative anatomy in the 1780's and to plant morphology in the 1790's produced insights of a comprehensive sort which were years in advance of the fields.

In a later chapter we shall turn to some of his contributions to science, but our approach to them has to begin much earlier, with the fundamental question as to where Goethe, child of the rationalistic, even pedantic Enlightenment, got his great faith in such an intuitive approach to nature, indeed, to understanding in general. Must we simply attribute it to an "artistic" temperament, thus begging a most fascinating question, or can we account for it biographically, i.e., in the development of his personality? Was there some field of inquiry where an intuitive approach led to experiences so satisfactory that he was encouraged to apply it elsewhere?

His first serious independent thinking occurred in the political sector, on precisely the same question of folk character which he was discussing with relish on the road to Venice. This had been the topic which most naturally interested him during his first experience abroad, in Strasbourg fifteen years earlier. At that time he had drawn conclusions about national character which had far-reaching implications for his entire youthful philosophy of life and especially for his concept of the artist, but also for his career as public servant in Weimar. The present chapter will pursue these lines of thought in the very young man. Since politics was a major concern in his years before Italy, we shall return to the topic again under the heading "political engagement," where it will at last offer a kind of transition to his scientific thinking.

If we wish to visualize the twenty-year-old as he arrived in Strasbourg in early April, 1770, we have to imagine an extremely thin, nervous youngster still recovering from a long bout with tuberculosis which had interrupted earlier studies in Leipzig. His face was narrow, he had a high forehead, his nose seemed especially prominent, his eyes unusually large and bright — a general appearance, incidentally, which the eighteenth century found attractive because it testified to sensitivity and otherworldiness. The boy suffered especially from loud noises, vertigo, and respiratory difficulties, as well as from that introspection which is often the result of protracted illness. Never before in his life — or afterward, either — had he so lacked self-confidence and self-sufficiency, but he was quite resolute about improving his constitution and impressing others that he was "a good fellow." He had a strong will, and on one of his first days in Strasbourg he climbed the cathedral tower in order to confront his dizziness and conquer it; in the same spirit he exposed his sensitive ears to marching bands. In the summer he actually undertook a trip by horseback from Strasbourg to Saarbrücken, and he seems to have enjoyed himself. Such fortunate ability to set his face to difficulties may have come from the influence of his father, who had shown great impatience with the sickly, somewhat hypochondriac son during his long convalescence. Now, away from his father, the boy conformed with and even exceeded the parental model which had so irritated him while at home.

He had given no sign of very original thinking yet, but he was quick-witted and exceptionally bright and inventive. He had by now fully assimilated rococo culture and enlightened philosophy. Among his own prolific literary accomplishments he could count a collection of lyrics as polished as any in the then popular Anacreontic style, which had been published together with musical scores. There were also at least two unpublished comedies after the French manner, not to speak of numerous other attempts which he now regarded as immature. The lyrics and the comedies alone would serve a modern student as a good introduction to the style and wit of middle-eighteenth-century Germany, including the inner contradictions of that epoch.

These contradictions are especially interesting, because they constitute the fault lines along which we are likely to discover any shift in taste and opinion just as soon as it begins to occur in intelligent heads. Writing poetry was a fashionable hobby for gentlemen, comparable perhaps to golfing for a modern well-to-do businessman. Although the mode dictated racy themes, no moral conflicts could arise as long as no one took the poems personally. Yet at the same time generally accepted theories about art insisted that it imitate "nature" closely. For a good while this contradiction did not disturb Goethe. He refers to the standard advanced opinion of his day, and in quibbling actually affirms it, when he sends a copy of his poems to a friend: "Well, here are my lyrics, and your good will toward me will treasure them more than they deserve — so I hope. The story of my heart painted in little miniatures! If ever poems did not conform with Batteaux' principle, then it is these: not a touch of imitation, all *is* nature. And therefore they will be eternal remembrances of my youth, for me and my friends."[9] Here is a young head which had adapted itself well to the opinions of the day, including the glib conventionalization of "nature." Can we really expect from it any serious original thinking about social, political, or cultural questions?

He is sure to have a ready command of current viewpoint on such matters. The all-male table at his Strasbourg boarding house constituted an audience for more serious discussions, and the general atmosphere at the university there was probably more settled and critical than in fashionable Leipzig. But most important for the development of Goethe's interests was his exceptional good fortune in meeting one of Europe's truly original thinkers just at this point, perhaps the most opportune time in his life for such an encounter. A busy summer in Strasbourg had prepared him for the comprehensive law examinations in the fall, and just about the time when he passed them and could find time for other interests, J. Gottfried Herder arrived in Strasbourg for a protracted stay.

Goethe learned certain new points of view from Herder and became acquainted with new authors through him, but more important was the fact that the boy recognized in the man, seven years older than he, the most powerful intellect he had yet come upon. He admired Herder tremendously: "If I am destined to be your satellite, then I will be, gladly and faithfully. A loving moon to the earth. But feel the entirety of this: that I would rather be Mercury, the last, or rather the least among seven that turn about one sun with you, than the first among five that revolve about Saturn. — Farewell, dear man. I will not release you. I will not! Jacob wrestled with the Angel of the Lord. Even if I should come away a cripple!"[10] Herder, on the other hand — and this, too, was a new experience for Goethe — received such outpourings with irony and even derision. How could he react otherwise to a glib dandy who had so facilely accommodated himself to fashionable mannerisms and to all the enlightened slogans which Herder wished to refute? "Goethe is really a good person, just very flighty, and much too flighty and sparrow-like — something which brought him my endless reproaches."[11]

This is from a letter to his fiancée after Herder had spent a few months with Goethe. He had come to Strasbourg just after meeting her, and while there had decided to break previous commitments in order to take a more permanent position which would permit him to marry. His guilty conscience on account of those commitments might have made him irritable with Goethe, but to this was added a kind of physical torment which we may be unable to imagine in our day of relatively painless medicine. In Strasbourg he had discovered a surgeon who promised to cure a chronically running eye in a matter of a few weeks, a prospect immensely attractive to a young man in love, despite the pain it entailed. A passageway was to be bored through from eye to nasal cavity, an opening cut in the tear duct, and these channels maintained until they became established in scar tissue. The operation turned out to be a failure and had to be repeated; the treatment dragged on for months and was ultimately unsuccessful. Goethe was a good-hearted boy who at first merely intended to brighten Herder's dismal waiting by conversation and reading. He soon found himself extremely eager to gain the man's approval, but for the first time in his life approval was extremely hard to come by. Herder's personality and the circumstances of their meeting thus turned out to be just as important for Goethe's development as were Herder's teachings.

Goethe wanted to have something to say on subjects of interest to his friend, but these lay mainly in the area of cultural history. It was a new topic for the younger man, one on which his thinking was being influenced by the locality. In Strasbourg he was abroad for the first time, confronted with national differences and apt to reflect on them. In better society French was spoken, although the dialect of the Alsatians was a German one. This discrepancy led him to look into their folkways, and he discovered there traditions with which a German could easily identify and even call "native," as distinct from the French ways of the more cultivated. A modern traveler gains some understanding of Goethe's reaction when he leaves children chattering Alsatian German on the streets and enters the French atmosphere of a Strasbourg cafe or business house. But it was also perfectly apparent — and sometimes stinging — to any young German of the eighteenth century that all the fashions, from clothes and hairstyles to literature and philosophy, flowed to Germany from France. How convenient to a young man who felt like rejecting the establishment, as is not very unusual among twenty-year-olds, if he could at the same time brand the establishment as foreign.

Strasbourg was a spot as if created for a young German to see the error of his rococo ways, and here it was that Goethe came to scorn the rational meliorism of the Enlightenment, with its faith in civilization and progress, as superficial and unworthy of his native tradition. As is always the case with the radical, however, it was easier for him to reject the establishment out of hand than to formulate in positive terms what should be set in its place. It is on this account that a radical is so liable to becoming reactionary.

Goethe turned to the German past to seek those permanent values which he would set against the specious accomplishments of civilization. His studies had required looking into the historical background of Germany's legal systems, and he attended extra lectures in European history. It may have been Herder who called his attention to the conservative pamphlets of an Osnabrück minister, Justus Möser, powerful champion of traditional usages and institutions inherited from the Middle Ages, which he praised in a manner anticipatory of the later Romantic generation. As in discussions with Herder, however, Goethe found in Möser no real system, not even any very specific ideas, but only a general understanding of national policy as something properly related to national character. This was quite different from the more explicit theories popular among leading intellectuals.

The professors to whom Goethe had listened uncritically in Leipzig had been liberal and Enlightened. They believed in the triumph of reason, the advancement of human knowledge, and social and economic progress. It was, after all, only the third quarter of the eighteenth century; none yet dreamed of the terrors to come in its final decade. The general assumption was that the paternally motivated hereditary rulers of the many little states would follow the examples set by Frederick II and his son Frederick Wilhelm II of Prussia, and by Maria Theresa and her son Joseph II of Austria; that they would accept the sane advice of their ministers from Germany's highly cultivated middle class, thereby knowing and implementing the best for their lands and people. In retrospect it seems difficult for us to quarrel with this view, for from our vantage point the petty principalities of Central Europe at mid-century appear to present one of the better governmental forms evolved in modern history. We have not since that era produced means of governing which are so close to the governed and so fully informed as to their needs, as well as responsive to them within the limits set by the character of the ruler and the means at his disposal. Certainly few other eras have been so indulgent of individual peculiarities, stubbornness, and eccentricity.

Even in his most vehement period Goethe never rejected the hereditary aristocracy and their rule, but he lashed out at any who might cavil at their privileges: "Will the tribe of poets and philosophers never comprehend that the aristocracy is our sole check against despotism? We would only desire that the true aristocracy might have a more intelligent education, and then we should happily suffer the distinction among the estates, which is so necessary to our way of life."[12] This is from a book review which he published in 1773, just about two years before he undertook the task of providing a "more intelligent education" for Carl August. He continued to regard the "distinction among the estates" as essential throughout his life. It was the intellectuals, the "tribe of poets and philosophers" and their speculative systems, that he railed against. "Genuine life," so goes a typical outburst of 1773, "leaves no room for speculation, and feeling leaves none for theorizing."[13] Although eighteenth-century thinkers believed the intellect competent in all areas, Goethe had perceived that rationalism is itself ultimately based on premises which are not subject to rational exposition. "There is nothing more pitiful than to hear people talk incessantly of reason while they act in accordance with prejudice alone. Nothing is so dear to them as tolerance, and their scorn of all opinions different from their own proves how little peace we can expect them to give us."[14] Since it is rationalism to which he is objecting, we shall scarcely expect the young fellow to offer us a rational system of his own. Still, it is possible for us to single out a few clear-cut issues on which he liked to dwell. He seemed to assume that the rightness of his stand on each has to be felt intuitively, and in its "entirety," or not at all.

Law and the history of law was naturally a recurrent concern of the law student. It was clear to him that the Roman code, to which he had devoted many a late hour, was quite different from Germanic common law. In his view the crucial distinction was that Roman codification represented a complex and systematic effort to make specific provision for all possible cases in advance, while common law made no such presumption on behalf of the intellect, but comprised instead relatively few traditionally honored and generally understood fundamentals. In accordance with them, ordinary men could make independent judgments in the light of precedent, local attitudes, and specific circumstance. Those who had introduced Roman law into Northern Europe had done so with their own advantage in mind. It had led to the exploitation of the lesser nobility — the backbone of the German system — and of the peasants. This is not to suggest that Goethe was a champion of the peasants or of social justice. The young anti-intellectual was interested solely in the cerebral issues. Especially revealing of his attitude is a scene from his drama *Götz von Berlichingen,* written in the fall of 1771, where Roman law is ridiculed as utopian.[15] It is defended by one Ölmann (not a pretty name, something like Greaseman in English) who has studied in Padua, there Latinized his name to Olearius, and is now helping the powerful Bishop of Bamberg to outmaneuver the honest folk by means of the strange and elaborate new legal system. Their victim is an embodiment of German genius, the hero Götz von Berlichingen.

Genius is another subject on which we are able to detect fairly clear-cut views on Goethe's part. Whereas an earlier generation had said *er hat Genie,* i.e., "He is witty and clever," it was now becoming more fashionable to say *er ist ein Genie,* "He is a genius." The famous critic Lessing, for example, used the word to mean an exceptionally gifted artist who could create in accordance with inspiration and without heed to the rules — Shakespeare was his favorite example. Herder tended to stress the importance of national character in developing the idea. A genius carried his own entire world in his breast; hence he was felt to "anticipate" nature without having to learn about her, much less imitate her. Reason constrains us to accumulate our information and our skills, and sees our accomplishments as contingent on learning; an *Originalgenie,* to use the popular slogan, produced something infinitely superior by responding to his impulses alone, because his work was in this way characteristic of himself and of his nation. In 1773 Goethe contributed a dithyramb on the Strasbourg Cathedral to a pamphlet that Herder edited. Here is an excerpt in which he condemns neoclassical architects: "You crept around upon the noble ruins begging their measurements, you patched your pleasure palaces together according to those sacred proportions and you think you have retained the secrets of art just because you can reduce the homes of giants to your own jot and tittle. If you had *felt* instead of measuring, if the spirit of those structures had descended upon you, you would not have been content merely to imitate, thinking it had to be beautiful because *they* did it that way. You would have created your own plans necessary and true, living beauty would have flowed, and taken form."[16]

Like the genius, a nation was also conceived as containing within itself all the laws governing its own development. Goethe insisted on treating nations as organisms which, to be understood at all, have to be met each on its own quite specific terms. He saw each folk as fundamentally different from every other, and he regarded genuine art as simple, pure expression of unique folk character. From this point of view it was absurd to

34

take the creations of any one people or epoch as standards for another, even such grand accomplishments as the Greek temple, Roman law, or French theater. When Goethe roamed around the Alsace collecting folksongs for Herder like the now famous lyric *Heidenröslein,* it was in accordance with this new concept of nationality, a conviction basically political in nature. If he did not hesitate to alter the songs he collected and even to compose new folk art, then this bespeaks his confidence that a native genius acts in full accord with his national character.

It goes without saying that the most reasonable political and social theories might be precisely the ones he found most repugnant to true folk character, which had to be sensed or, as he put it, "felt in its entirety." Quite maddening to the young anti-rationalist was his recognition that reason and civilization are indeed capable of bridging national differences.

As soon as a nation is polished, as soon as it has conventionalized ways of thinking, behaving and perceiving, it ceases to possess character. The aggregate of individual perceptions and their thrust, the specific philosophy of life and its influence on these perceptions — such are the features which go to make up the character of living systems. And how much of all that is retained by polished nations? The implications of religion and those civil issues inseparable from them, the pressure of the law, the yet greater pressure of social institutions, and a thousand other matters prevent the polished man and the polished nation from ever being themselves, they silence the voice of nature and wash out every feature which might contribute to a characteristic image.[17]

If we are to despise our civilized institutions and cannot even trust our conscious intellect, where then shall we turn for direction in public matters? To judge from *Götz von Berlichingen* and from *Egmont,* the other political drama Goethe conceived in the early 1770's, he thought that a people desires to be guided and is, in fact, best led by the intuitive right thinking of its "great" sons, those whose personalities are best in accord with national character. In the eighteenth century this was tantamount to saying that a nation can best be expected to develop organically under the rule of its local aristocracy. Goethe never argued that he was offering an ideal solution; his position was precisely that no utopian ideals should be entertained. Changes recommended by political theoreticians in the service of some intellectual scheme are best compared with changes imposed by a conquering foreign power in its own national interest.

Even though the younger generation greeted *Götz von Berlichingen* enthusiastically for its political and cultural implications, Goethe's purpose had not been to convey a deliberate "message." He wished to capture what he took to be a characteristic situation: a "great" individual succumbs to the general baseness of his era. The play is set in the early sixteenth century, a time when the more powerful German princes were expanding their territory at the expense of the lesser estates and of the emperor. The feud of an independent knight of the empire with one of these great princes, and his inevitable defeat, constitute the plot of what Goethe at first called a "history dramatized." Its philosophy of history is an adaptation of Rousseau's cultural pessimism to Herder's ideas of nationality. Goethe explicitly associates decline in national character with erosion of traditional values in the advance of civilization. The process becomes apparent in conflicts like Götz's, where a man born to lead succumbs instead to the trend of history. Such junctures as these constitute the true moments of tragedy, as Goethe explained when analyzing Shakespeare's work: "when the assumed freedom of our will collides with the necessary gravitation of the mass."[18] *Götz von Berlichingen* was conceived as a tragedy in this sense, and not as a political manifesto.

Goethe even revised it in an attempt to make it less "con-

trived," presumably to let the historical argument recede in favor
of dramatic interest. As a consequence some of the outbursts most
revealing of his political, ethical, and cultural stands were deleted.
"Reflection is a disease of the mind and has led only to diseased
actions," says Götz's closest friend. "Doing good is a noble virtue, but it is the privilege of the strong. Those who because they
are soft-hearted continually do good, do good, are no better than
people who can't hold their urine," says his wife. Götz himself
thinks he will know that God has opened the eyes of the great
"when they feel the extreme rapture of partaking in their subjects' happiness; when they find human heart enough to taste
the bliss of being a great man; when their well-tended, blessed
land seems to them a paradise instead of their artificial, clipped
recluse gardens; when the full check, the joyous expression of each
peasant with his large family assures the fat of their peaceful land
and, compared with this sight, all their theaters and art galleries
leave them cold." Revision also dramatized the lines of action, so
that personal intrigues come more to the fore than historical
trends. Neither of the play's versions can really make a claim to
artistic eminence, and the earlier has the merit of spontaneity.
Nevertheless, the fact of the revision speaks for Goethe's motives
in that it shows his intention to have been primarily an artistic
one.

When he and a friend printed and distributed the revised *Götz*
at their own expense in 1773, they probably thought of it as a
kind of calling card for the ruling houses in German lands. No
work could have struck the German nobility as more flattering,
and in recent decades they had shown themselves interested in at-
tracting authors to their courts, sometimes simply in the capacity
of favorites (Voltaire in Berlin), frequently as tutors to young
princes (Wieland in Weimar), but also to some especially appropriate office (like Lessing's librarianship in Brunswick) and even
in outright ministerial service (Möser in Osnabrück), although

seldom to pursue their art quite independently (as Klopstock did in Denmark). When a Weimar chamberlain, himself a poet and translator, brought his two young princes to visit Goethe toward the end of 1774, the main subjects of their conversations appear to have been *Götz* and the political ideas of Justus Möser. One of these princes was Carl August, within six months of his majority, marriage, and accession to rule in Saxe-Weimar.

His interest in Goethe, an idol of his generation who was at the same time an outspoken advocate of views on the aristocracy marvelously to the taste of an absolute ruler still wet behind the ears, is easy to understand. A duke just come to power could scarcely accomplish a more brilliant stroke in the cultural realm than acquisition of this particular author. In November, 1775, came the first step, Goethe's invitation to Weimar for interview purposes. There was little question about the willingness of the influential members of the court to indulge an *Originalgenie* for a time, anyhow; the more important consideration was achieving a favorable impression on Goethe. Hence he had to wait for the new ducal coach being delivered by Carl August's most promising associate, the son of President of the Chamber von Kalb, in whose house Goethe was lodged. The younger von Kalb was about Goethe's age, and there was a pretty daughter.

Goethe was flattered by familiar association with the aristocracy, for whom at this late time in their history it had become camp to look upon the middle class as equals. The irony of it seems still to have gone unnoticed by all. In sweet condescension, not in arrogant presumption, Marie Antoinette was playing milkmaid in Versailles, and it was with a similar thrill that the lords and ladies in Weimar seated themselves at the same table with this middle-class Frankfurter — they contrived it by arranging to have a member of their card party called away in the middle of a round, so that Goethe, waiting at an appointed distance, could replace him. The familiarity with the duke went far indeed, farther, no doubt, than Goethe would have permitted had he been less intoxicated by the attentions of so many great personages. But they, after all, expected unconventionality in an *Originalgenie,* and it was in this capacity that he was to regale the court through a typically dreary rural winter. He recited his own brilliant poetry, much of it — like *Faust* — as yet unpublished. He set up an amateur theater in which the nobility could themselves take the stage, something indeed titillating. He visited all the important houses and let himself be shown off at neighboring courts. When the ponds froze over, he encouraged the Weimaraners in the new poetic fad of ice skating.

Carl August, so recently tied to the apronstrings of his mother's regency and under the thumb of her sage advisers, was completely carried away by his charming and versatile guest. He neglected his bride scandalously, often sleeping with Goethe even while at court, and he was always eager to make an excursion into the countryside with boisterous comrades. Goethe was himself by no means yet so staid as to maintain complete self-control as he came to realize that he held virtually absolute sway over a boy whose wish was the law of Saxe-Weimar. He probably resolved at an early point to stay on and take a taste of political power (although a decision was not reported home to Frankfurt until after New Year's, nor accepted — grudgingly — by Weimar's officialdom until summer). It is doubtful that he looked upon Weimar as a permanent arena. Who could know how far genius and good fortune might yet take him? To judge by his successes in these first few months, very far indeed.

By the beginning of 1776 it was clear to all concerned that the interview was over and that Goethe's tenure as favorite of the duke was to be indefinite. However, the exact nature of his position remained in contention between Carl August and his ministers throughout the spring. Goethe's first major political success was announced in February. The general superintendency of public worship (this included the schools) was to be offered to the unorthodox cultural philosopher Gottfried Herder. We know that Carl August considered this appointment a victory over his conservative clerics; it is difficult to imagine what a triumph it must have meant for Goethe with this one coup both to make the fortune of the hero of his youth and to shape the spiritual course of a land for decades to come, as he surely felt, for the better. In March he secured a further appointment, that of Corona Schröter, a beautiful actress whom he had adored in his student days in Leipzig. About this time he moved out of the von Kalb house into his own rented quarters, but Carl August was also expropriating a cottage and garden for him at a secluded yet convenient point on the Ilm River, which flows past the castle. In early June the favorite was at last accorded an official title, granted an income reported to be in the improbably high neighborhood of a thousand taler (in fact, it was twelve hundred), and installed as a member of the Privy Council with a vote.

That ruling princes should have boudoir counselors and even be strongly swayed by them was a fact of life to which government circles of the period were generally resigned. The Privy Council, however, as the highest administrative authority, constituted the last practical check on a prince's arbitrary judgments and rash actions. Goethe's appointment to one of its three seats seemed highly improper to serious officials who had devoted a lifetime to the affairs of the duchy. The senior member of the council was quite set on resigning — and that would have well pleased Carl August, who was eager for a clean sweep — but the plea of the third member not to be left alone with young firebrands, together with the eloquent intervention of the dowager duchess, persuaded him to stay on. Thus a perhaps serious crisis in government was averted.

It had been a brilliant six-month performance for Goethe, not without its dangerous and questionable aspects. From our remove and even from his own maturer, retrospective view, Weimar appears small and unimportant in the context of European history. But in those days it was a question of Weimar's importance in the context of a young man's career. It was one of the ruling houses of the civilized world, Carl August a nephew of Frederick, already being called the Great. The role of favorite at any one of these houses was played before the eyes of all Europe on a stage where stirring drama was accustomed fare. Perhaps the most celebrated court tragedy had in fact been enacted very recently by the favorite of Denmark's psychotic Christian VII, Johann Friedrick Struensee. It was so familiar to Goethe and his contemporaries that it should be outlined here.

Struensee had been a penurious physician in that German-speaking area then a part of Denmark, until his radical political views cemented a friendship with an out-of-favor nobleman, Schock-Karl von Rantzau-Ascheberg. Von Rantzau helped establish Struensee among aristocratic circles. His handsome presence and psychological finesse brought him quick success, and in 1768 he obtained a position as one of the physicians to Christian VII. He soon gained the complete confidence of this mentally ill young man, convincing him that the royal authority ought to be absolute and unimpeded by governmental agencies. Although the queen was at first unfriendly, he gained her favor, too, by persuading the effeminate Christian to give her a measure of recognition. In all likelihood by the spring of 1770 Struensee had become her lover. The king seemed to encourage the relationship, while Struensee and the queen flaunted it for all to see. It was not at all a case of immorality among the decadent, but something beyond that: a highly rational man of superior morals felt that he was above mere conventionality.

Possessed of absolute power in Denmark, Struensee rapidly developed into a kind of caricature of the Enlightenment, in whom its best as well as its worst features came to stand out with great clarity. Within a matter of months he had advanced Danish society a hundred and fifty years ahead of the rest of Europe. His incredibly successful measures constituted a kind of catalogue of the noblest eighteenth-century theories. Privileges and offices of the nobility were cut back brutally, and numerous abuses were done away with peremptorily. The military was reduced radically, the national economy rationalized with no heed to vested interest, incompetence turned out of office, and new appointments made — with uncanny aptness — on the basis of merit alone. Lingering vestiges of serfdom were eradicated, public welfare and even public health measures were undertaken (large-scale vaccination against smallpox, for example, still suspiciously rejected by many in Europe), the penal system was reformed, harsh punishments and torture were abolished, the puritanical laws governing public morality were repealed and the people were granted entertainment instead, from music at the squares on Sunday to government-inspected brothels. Energetic and resolute, Struensee took Frederick of Prussia as his model in holding tight reins, basing his measures on first-hand knowledge and checking personally on their execution.

It is conceivable that he might have remained long in power, becoming a kind of Danish Cromwell and radically altering the course of European history, had it not been for a few errors so fundamental that they were surely inseparable from the thinking which led to his remarkable reforms. They are especially interesting to us because they illustrate in an exaggerated way those negative aspects of the Enlightenment which most galled Goethe in his youth. Struensee spoke only German — he had not time, he said, to learn Danish. His attitude was the same toward national institutions and traditions. His theories, after all, were universally valid, and nationality seemed to him just another vested interest standing in the way of progress. His greatest single offense to the Danes may well have been the abolition of the Royal

Danish Guard as nonfunctional and uneconomical. That it was a source of great national pride was of no consequence to him. Similarly, his incorruptible economies at court undermined Copenhagen industry, much of it directly dependent on royal and aristocratic frivolities. In his rational single-mindedness, he alienated one by one every segment of Danish society: the church, the aristocracy, the military, the middle class, even his own efficient appointees, whom he overworked by never permitting them a sense of security. His old patron Rantzau, unable to make any deals with Struensee, at last went over to the ever growing opposition. As early as 1772 it was an easy matter to organize a conspiracy against the king and his favorite. In January an efficient palace revolution introduced a new, conservative era in Denmark and a deep-seated rejection of all things German. Struensee was executed in February.

His rise to power had coincided with Goethe's months in Strasbourg and is sure to have been a major topic at table; while Struensee was pushing his reforms to their logical extremes, Goethe was writing *Götz von Berlichingen*. How much his thinking at the time might be a reaction to Struensee's particular brand of liberalism is only a matter of interesting conjecture. It is certain, however, that those who watched Goethe's rapid rise in Weimar had all been influenced by the scandal in Denmark, and it is against this background that we can best appreciate their fears as well as Goethe's own constant references to a "political drama" in which he was playing a dangerous role. "I am now fully embarked on the wave of the world, firmly resolved to discover, to win, to fight, to crash — or to blow myself and my whole cargo into the air."[19]

That is not mere rhetoric. Had he fallen from favor or, what was more likely, had some accident befallen Carl August, there were many at court eager to take advantage of the favorite's vulnerable position. He had been gulled by an eighteen-year-old's conception of an *Originalgenie,* and the very best interpretation which we are able to place on the wild doings of the first Weimar winter and spring is that this Falstaff surely had a pedagogical end in view with his Prince Hal. The memoirs and outraged letters which have come down to us must be exaggerated, but they cannot be entirely without foundation. There are recollections of drunken parties, wine bottles flung at fleeing guests, windows smashed out with silver talers. Goethe encouraged the hitherto sheltered boy to spend a great deal of time in the villages and among his foresters and gamekeepers — something perhaps in itself irregular in the *ancien régime* — and it is undoubtedly true that they occasionally camped in the forest, sharing simple fare, but it is also reported that they shared the same girls. Goethe popularized swimming among the courtiers, a sport so rare among their class that nakedness probably made it no worse, but shall we also believe that Carl August and eight or ten comrades would jump out and dance rings around passing girls and preachers? That he and Goethe popped bull whips on the town square at daybreak seems attested (Goethe injured an eye in this way), but did they really set up the Bible as target for pistol practice? Did they tie the skirts of a respectable Weimar citizen over her head? Apparently we can be sure only that Goethe and an enthusiastic disciple made outdoor exercise like riding, swimming, boxing, stilt-walking, even rope-walking popular in Weimar for a time at least, that they also enjoyed horseback excursions through the duchy and mingling, sometimes incognito, with the common folk. Excessive boisterousness must have occurred often, but it is not clear to what extent Goethe was responsible for it, or merely an unwilling follower. We know that in later years he used his influence to restrain the maturer but scarcely less impetuous duke in his predilection for the destructive and dangerous, but most observers in 1776 could see no further than the favor which a newcomer was currying with their rash young ruler, and they

44

connected it with his unconventional behavior. The tales that they spread reflect accurately, if not the facts, certainly the just outrage of the orthodox.

Carl August and Goethe are said to have called on an old peasant woman late one evening, giving themselves out as hunters. While she fetched them some milk to drink, they coaxed her tomcat into the churn. On a subsequent visit Carl August gave the old woman a gold piece to make up for her loss. She was at first astonished at such a gift from a hunter, but then she pocketed the coin, winked and took him into her confidence: "I sent the butter to court. They'll put up with anything there." The anecdote is probably apocryphal, but it does illustrate one point well enough: just what recourse do you have if the lord of the land ruins your butter? How do you defend yourself when a ruling prince bangs on your door in the middle of your wedding night and rips the expensive new wallpaper with his saber because he finds it "philistine"? If there is no appeal, then it follows that the absolute ruler must be especially nice in observing proprieties. However exaggerated the gossip, Carl August was by no means meticulous in that 1776 springtime, and the burden of blame rests on Goethe, if only because of his seniority and influence. He knew this and in later years regretted his participation. Perhaps he regretted it at the time.

The famous poet Klopstock, who had followed his patron, the Danish foreign minister, back to Germany after Struensee removed him from office, felt that his own highly respected position in German letters, the cordial relationship which he had established with Goethe the previous year, and his own bitter personal experience in Copenhagen all constituted an obligation on his part to write to Goethe and remind him that the reputation of German authors was sure to suffer from such gossip as that current from Weimar. "Spare us such letters in the future dear Klopstock. They effect no good, and they do bring us a few unhappy moments. You are yourself aware that I have no answer. Either I would have to chime *pater peccavi* like a schoolboy, seek excuses like a sophist, or stand up for my honor like a good chap, and the result would be a mixture of all three — but to what purpose? So, not another word between us on the subject. Believe me, it would take every moment of my existence if I answered all such letters, all such admonitions."[20] The friendship with Klopstock was permanently destroyed.

The first epoch in Goethe's political development comes to a close with his move to Weimar. His thinking about politics was still very immature in 1776, going little farther than his youthful stroke of intuition in Strasbourg. If we find it fraught with inconsistencies, we must at least give him credit for departing from the orthodox channels with which the lecture hall had familiarized him. Furthermore, he himself disclaimed any rational basis for his political notions. Their weakest point was precisely on the issue which is popularly assumed to constitute the entirety of politics: the machinery of government. This is the area where Goethe could be expected to refine his thinking as soon as he became involved in the details of administration.

It should not be forgotten that all notions of government rest ultimately upon our concept of the governed. It is remarkable how little Goethe's view of the *folk* changed after 1770. His experience in administration forced him to temper and at last relinquish his idealization of the hereditary ruler, but it did not alter his idea of characteristic nationality. He perceived Venice, for example, as "a grand, awe-inspiring work of collective human energy, a magnificent monument not of a ruler, but of a folk."[21] The nation as an organic entity whose unique character had to be grasped intuitively was never rejected by Goethe; the Weimar years only confirmed that early perception and invested it with more immediate meaning for him. Thus a political notion becomes our earliest example of a typically Goethean mode of

46

thought. Subsequent experience was interpreted in such a way as to confirm his "first sure insight," and he continued, consciously and eventually programmatically, to rely on the intuitive flash in other areas of endeavor as well. Before following the development of his speculative thinking, however (in the chapters "Political Engagement" and "Nature Studies"), we shall try to get better acquainted with some other sides of his personality.

NOTES

1. Diary, September 22, 1786.
2. Diary, September 29, 1786, for example.
3. Diary, October 4, 1786.
4. To Herder on December 30, 1786.
5. To Charlotte on December 29, 1786.
6. He called first impressions "a mixture of truth with a high degree of deception" in his diary, September 24, 1786.
7. June 18, 1795.
8. Diary, February 26, 1780.
9. To Langer in mid-October, 1769. *DjG* 1, 280.
10. Fall, 1771. *DjG* 2, 69.
11. Herder to Caroline Flachsland on March 21, 1772. Grumach 1, 171.
12. Review of *Vorzüge des alten Adels* for the *Frankfurter Gelehrte Zeitung*. *DjG* 3, 91.
13. Review of *Allgemeine deutsche Bibliothek*, *DjG* 3, 98.
14. *Brief des Pastors....JA* 36, 86.
15. *Der bischöfliche Palast in Bamberg.*
16. *Von deutscher Baukunst. JA* 33, 4 f.
17. Review for the *Frankfurter Gelehrte Anzeigen. JA* 36, 70.
18. *Zum Schakespears Tag* (October, 1771). *JA* 36, 5 f.
19. To Lavater on March 6, 1776.
20. May 21, 1776.
21. Diary, September 29, 1786.

Questions about Individuality

W<small>E</small> conjectured that the attentions Goethe received in Carlsbad from those who remembered him as the author of *Werther* may have caused him to think about editing and publishing his works. He had not done so before because of his aversion to taking money for what he called his "children." His pen had never "fattened his soup, will not and shall not," he had somewhat tactlessly told the novelist Sophie de la Roche.[1] Yet the terrific financial uncertainty connected with his upcoming Italian trip brought about a change in this attitude. When Weimar's sole capitalist, Friedrich Bertuch, approached him in May, 1786, about underwriting an edition with the enterprising young Leipzig publisher Göschen, Goethe not only acceded but drove a hard bargain. For eight volumes he demanded, and got, the then exceptionally handsome honorarium of two thousand taler, to be paid as the material was delivered. He said he could offer two volumes immediately, two more by the fall book fair, and the last four at Easter of the next year. It was a schedule he could not even approximately hold to, for he had involved himself in the most psychologically exacting task of his life.

A first approach to it evoked the protest that he would not "go through these things and renew them" in himself if he didn't have to. "Many old sores" were being opened up, and examining them was painful.[2] Most discouraging was his feeling that his poetic career might have ended. "I resolved to print my fragments at a time when I thought I was dead," he admitted later. "How happy I shall be when I can validate the fact that I am alive again by completing the things I have begun."[3] In the agreement with Göschen he promised to do his best to finish numerous incomplete pieces which were advertised for the last four volumes. He was obviously looking toward Italy for the leisure time to do so, and even for the inspiration. When he told Carl August that he was going away "to improve all kinds of failings and to fill all kinds of lacunae," he had, above all else, his creative ability in mind.[4]

The first four of the eight volumes presented only two major problems. *Iphigenia* of Volume III required significant revision, so that he decided to take the manuscript with him to Rome. Volume I was to contain *Werther,* that novel with which the world associated his name and which had been sufficiently autobiographical in the psychological crisis it detailed that he, too, felt a strong personal attachment to the work. In the early 1780's he had already attempted a revision; now in Carlsbad in the summer of 1786 he set about finishing it. He had the help of the friend of his youth, Herder, who also planned to represent him with the publisher as later volumes were sent in.

In general, Goethe approached *Werther* with restraint, only here and there attempting to bring out the thought of the original more clearly with short additions or delicate rearrangements. This is noteworthy, because there was much about the novel which embarrassed him now — "The author made a mistake in not shooting himself when he finished writing it," he observed as he took up the task.[5] He was willing to use great care and even tenderness in opening these channels of understanding back into a period when he had been most preoccupied with questions about his own identity. It was that same period in which he wrote *Götz,*

49

but while the drama had dealt with largely intellectual issues, *Werther* treated extremely personal ones.

At the Imperial Chancery Court in Wetzlar an ambitious young clerk, J. Christian Kestner, was so conscientious as to prepare several drafts of his letters. The second draft of one written in 1772 can best introduce us to the *Werther* period:

> Last spring there arrived here a certain Goethe from Frankfurt who calls himself Doctor of Law, twenty-three years old, sole son of a very rich father, with the purpose of gaining legal experience. This was his father's intention, his own being to study Homer, Pindar, and whatever else his "genius," i.e., his own way of thinking, and his heart might inspire him to do.
>
> Right at the outset the local intellectual set acclaimed him publicly as one of their ilk and as a collaborator in the new *Frankfurter Gelehrte Zeitung,* also, incidentally, as a *philosophe,* and they were at pains to associate themselves with him. Since I do not belong among this sort, or, rather, do not circulate so freely, I became acquainted with Goethe only later and quite by accident. One of our leading intellectuals, *Legations Sekretär* Gotter, had persuaded me to accompany him on his customary walk to the village of Garbenheim. There I found him lying in the grass under a tree, on his back, conversing with some people standing round about, an Epicurean (the great genius Goue), a stoic (Kielmannsegge), and a mixture of both (Dr. König), enjoying himself very well. Afterward he said he was much pleased that I had encountered him for the first time in such circumstances. Many things, some of them interesting, were under discussion. For the present I made no further judgment than: he is not an uninteresting person. You know that I do not form hasty judgments. I did conclude that he had wit and a lively imagination, but this was not yet enough to win my esteem.
>
> Before I continue, I must attempt a depiction of him which is based on our subsequent, close acquaintance.

He has very many gifts, and is a true genius as well as a man of character. He possesses an extraordinarily lively imagination and expresses himself for the most part in images and metaphors. His own opinion is that he always expresses himself figuratively and is not capable of literal expression, but hopes that when he is older he can both think and speak his thoughts as they are.

All his passions are violent, but he often has much self-control. He is noble minded and hence he acts free of prejudice, in accordance with impulse, never worrying about whether it pleases others, or is fashionable, or whether etiquette permits it. He hates all artificiality. . . .[6]

Kestner now rather pedantically goes into the philosophical and religious outlook of the young man with whom he and his fiancee, Charlotte Buff, became better acquainted as the summer of 1772 progressed. Since Kestner was working single-mindedly toward the day when marriage would be possible, Lotte found more time for their flighty but charming friend, and Goethe was just of an age and disposition to become enamored of her. It was an unusual sort of infatuation. The character of the relationship and Goethe's pathos are apparent from the notes which he left behind him when, in the early morning hours of September 11, he abruptly departed Wetzlar. If they strike us as notes written at death's brink, it is because the three had indulged in sentimental discussions of the hereafter until late the previous evening, at which time Goethe went back to his room and wrote: "He is gone, Kestner! When you get this note, he is gone. Give the enclosed message to Lotte. I had been very composed, but your conversation tore me apart. At this moment I am able to tell you no more than: Farewell! Had I stayed on for one moment more I would not have been able to control myself. Now I am alone, tomorrow I go. Oh, my poor head." To Charlotte: "Oh, I hope to return, but God knows when. Oh Lotte, what a state my heart was in while you were talking, when I knew that I was with you for the last time — not the last time! But I am going tomorrow. He is gone!

"Whatever could have brought you onto *that* topic, just at a time when I was unable to hold back my feelings?"

We can only conjecture about the scene which had occurred. Goethe seems to be toying with the notion of suicide. He continues: "Now I am alone, and I can weep. I leave you two happy, and I shall remain in your hearts. And I shall see you again — but to see you tomorrow is the same as never. Tell my boys [Lotte's younger brothers] he is gone. I can't go on." A few hours later: "I am packed, Lotte, and day is breaking. In another quarter hour I shall be gone. I forgot my sketches. Divide them among the children. . . . It must be thus: after 'today, tomorrow and the day-after-tomorrow' I cannot add what I often, in jest, did add. . . ." His quotation is from Rousseau's popular novel *Eloise*. It continues: "and all my life."

Young love is apt to be a remarkable mixture of passion, fancy, and idealism. Goethe saw considerably more in Kestner's Lotte than a less imaginative youth might have found. She was the eldest of a large, motherless brood, and his favorite memory was of coming upon her as she distributed bread and sausage among her brothers and sisters. He fancied he saw Mother Nature, lavish with her many children — in Lotte wonderfully merged with the bride who has eyes for only one of the many, singled out for his unique worth. Separated from Kestner and Lotte, idealization of the reality became all the more elaborate and attractive.

A lively correspondence between Wetzlar and Frankfurt tells us a great deal about this development, because the young Goethe was so astonishingly open about his feelings, weaving them into artistically composed letters like this one:

Golden Lotte, I thank whatever benevolent spirit prompted you to send me the surprise — I would be thankful even to a spirit black as fate. I said a warm hello to your picture before

going to dinner today, and the unusually thick envelope from
you was waiting for me at the table. I opened it and — put it
away again. Oh, dear Lotte, how things have changed since
first I saw you! This bow ribbon still has the very same blossom
color, but now it seems paler than it did in the coach that day.
It is understandable. I thank your heart that you are still able
to send me a present of this sort. Yet at the same time, in the
darkest recesses of my misery, I — No, Lotte, I have not lost
you. May the sweetest fruits of the abundance of Heaven be
yours. In Paradise, where cool brooks flow beside palm trees and
where fruits hang down like gold, may he to whom they are
denied here below find — at the moment I would be content
with just one hour with you.[7]

The summer's flirtation with Lotte Buff was one among several
dalliances with an ideal of the feminine contribution to masculine
existence. Goethe's hope that she returned his affection derived
mainly from his strong need to be appreciated. "Sometimes
doubts arise in me, and I think of Lotte in a big hooped skirt like
all the rest — but soon I see her again in her blue striped house-
dress and in her ingenuous sweetness that singles her out from all
the rest: and then I hope that in her soul I will not be lost
among the great number."[8] When he came to write *Werther,* he
by no means forgot that blossom-colored bow ribbon which Lotte
had sent him, but made of it a striking symbol for the importance
of an individual among the great number:

I kiss this bow a thousand times and, with every breath, I drink
in the remembrance of those abounding raptures, of those few
happy, irrecoverable days. . . . The blossoms of life are ephem-
eral. How many pass away without leaving a trace behind!
How few develop into fruit! And how few of these ever reach
maturity! But still there are plenty. Yet, oh my brother, can
we neglect *ripened fruits,* let them wither and rot, despised and
untasted?

Farewell. It is a magnificent summer. I often sit up in the fruit trees in Lotte's orchard with the longhandled fruit-picker and pluck pears out of the top. She stands on the ground and takes them as I hand them down.[9]

Werther's Lotte is also betrothed, and Werther saves himself from despair by fleeing as fall approaches.

On that fine September morning of 1772, Goethe left Wetzlar to take a journey on foot and by boat down the lovely Lahn River valley to Ems, where he spent several days in the lavish home of Madame de la Roche and her two handsome, dark-haired daughters. They were of the nobility, but far from snubbing their middle-class house guest, these were just the ladies who best knew how to appreciate the passion of a sentimental young man for a maiden who could never in this world requite it. When he returned to Frankfurt, however, he wrote to Madame de la Roche that it was "the fate of the noblest of souls to pine in vain for a mirror of themselves."[10] Goethe had encountered at home one of his first really difficult experiences, the announced engagement of his sister.

Cornelia* was his only sibling to survive beyond childhood. She idolized her brother and encouraged his writing. When older, he characterized their close relationship (they were just a little over a year apart) in a remarkable manner:

> During the early years brother and sister shared everything, play and study, growth and development, until they came to look on one another as twins. Sharing and mutual trust continued into that period when our physical and moral natures emerge, when the awe of youth at the awakening of sensual drives lends them spiritual character and visualizes spiritual needs in sensual imagery, when reflection on our condition rather enshrouds us than enlightens us, in the way a mist will cover a glen out of which it is about to rise and does not illuminate it. Hand in hand, brother and sister shared and endured

*Subjects marked with asterisks appear in the illustration section.

Goethe in Switzerland. Jens Juel, 1779.

Cornelia. Goethe, ca. 1770.

Fritz. Goethe, 1777.

Botanical notes from Italy. Goethe, after 1786.

The Beloved of the *Roman Elegies*. Goethe, ca. 1788.

Capitoline Hill. Goethe, 1787.

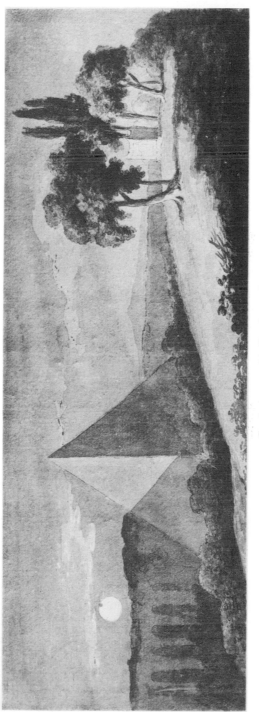

Cestius' pyramid. Goethe, 1787.

Goethe after Italy. Johann Heinrich Meyer, 1794.

their many errors and confusions, unable to enlighten themselves about their remarkable condition because whenever they looked to each other for knowledge the sacred reserve of their close kinship held them sternly apart.[11]

He goes on to express his regret that he never wrote anything which bore "the imprint of her personality," but his memory surely was failing him here. This sister, unattractive to men and fearful of them, in a constantly strained relationship with her father, and later with her husband, so lavished affection and understanding on her brother that her "image in his soul" is reflected in many of his works, not only in those from the Frankfurt years when she was the first to encourage and applaud his writing, but also in the years after he lost her. Particularly in his early twenties, when questions pertaining to the importance of his individual personality were uppermost in his mind, Cornelia's high opinion of her only brother was indispensable to his self-esteem.

Her engagement constituted a difficult emotional crisis for Goethe. The opening epistle in *Werther* gives us some idea of its seriousness:

Oh, that the sweetheart of my youth is gone! Oh, that I ever knew her! I might say: you are a fool, seeking what cannot be found here below. But I did have her. I have felt that heart, that magnificent soul whose presence increased my opinion of myself because my full potential was realized when I was with her. Good God, was a single gift in my soul neglected, was I not able to unfold before her the entire wonderful feeling with which my heart embraces nature, was not our togetherness an eternal intertwining of the subtlest sensibility and the sharpest intellect, of which the variations — even the aberrations — were stamped with the mark of genius?

This vision of "how I would like to be loved" was one that Goethe pursued for a good part of his life. It came close to realization in the mystical bond with the Lady Charlotte von Stein and may at last have been fulfilled during his sixties, when a late love affair found expression in mutual poetry. The *Werther* mood is set by unattainable love and want of understanding from the beloved one.

Not long after Goethe had left Wetzlar, he heard rumor that a friend there (Goue) had committed suicide. He wrote to Kestner, eager for details and eager to express himself on the subject: "I do honor such an act. It causes me to weep for all mankind. Let the whoreson philistines make their wise, tobacco-smoke remarks about it and say, 'I told you so.' I hope never to trouble *my* friends with such news."[12] Suicide and talk of suicide was quite the vogue just in those days. Only three weeks later another Wetzlar acquaintance, the son of a famous Protestant minister, named Jerusalem, did in fact shoot himself. It was said that the young man was in love with a married woman and had also suffered social rebuffs in his professional life. Goethe again asked Kestner for details, again expressing himself vehemently:

> Those shameful people who enjoy naught but vanity's chaff, with idolatrous lust in their hearts preach idolatry, restrain righteous nature, incite our energies and frustrate them at the same time — let those devils bear the blame for this tragedy, for *our* tragedy. May their brother the devil take them! If his father the damned preacher is not the guilty one, then let God forgive me my wish that he break his neck like Eli. The poor boy! When I was coming back from a walk and met him in the moonlight I said to myself: he is in love. Lotte surely remembers how I smiled at the thought. God knows loneliness is what ate out his heart.[13]

This outrage against the elder Jerusalem, whom Goethe did not even know, spills out into railing at the older generation in general and probably reveals Goethe's impatience with his own father. In these same days he wrote of him: "Dear God, when

I get old shall I become that way, too? Will my soul no longer attach itself to what deserves my love and is good? It is remarkable how people can believe that a man as he grows older becomes freer of what is of this earth, and petty."[14] Goethe not only resented the man who had "given" Cornelia to her fiance; he was openly hostile to his entire situation in Frankfurt, where his father had set him up in a law practice for which he felt no calling. Had the elder Goethe been established himself, the son might have had an opportunity to perform with distinction and to take some personal satisfaction and pride in the law. As it was, the old man lived well from his inheritance while his son served the shabbiest of clientele (as a young lawyer often must), mostly petty squabblers from the Frankfurt ghetto. Young Dr. Goethe certainly saw neither basis nor prospect for distinction in such a context, although his use of the title "Doctor" — the degree had not been conferred on him — bespeaks his wish for respectability. There even survives evidence that he did not remain in utter obscurity as a lawyer. Now we find that a judge must call him to order for flamboyant style; now a friend reminds him that it is the client, not the advocate, who should come off well in the eyes of the magistrate.

But in the law office there would never be recognition of his individuality; here he would pass for one of the undistinguished mass. It was as an artist that he felt he had his only hope of achieving any distinction. According to his autobiography, an important decision in favor of writing as opposed to painting occurred on that same walk down the Lahn as he left Wetzlar, and he was casting about for more subjects which, like *Götz*, might lead to a less conventional treatment than the plays of his student years. He probably had a literary use in mind when he wrote to Kestner for details about the two suicide reports, sensing that this was a promising topic for him and for the time. As it happened, Jerusalem had borrowed Kestner's pistols on the pretext that he was planning a trip, and with these weapons he had taken his life. Kestner's characteristically meticulous account of the suicide eventually found its way virtually unedited into the final pages of *Werther*. Goethe seems to have been convinced that he had here a case with which many in his age group would identify: "A noble heart and a highly intelligent mind, how easily strong emotional experiences can bring them to a decision of this sort."[15]

In confirming receipt of Kestner's report, Goethe volunteered the joking assurance: "I'll not shoot myself anytime soon."[16] It is not unusual for a young man to toy with the notion of taking his life, or to hint at it thus. Goethe at some time did a great deal of thinking about suicide, as is clear from *Werther*. One of Werther's letters tells us that in "ordinary existence" most men have to deceive themselves from one day to the next. Even the person who does not thus cajole himself clings to life. "Yet, hemmed in as he is, he cherishes in his heart the sweet feeling of freedom, that he can leave this dungeon whenever he will."[17] The novel tries to treat the subject of suicide — at the time an extremely controversial one — sympathetically and analytically. "Human nature," says Werther, "has its limits. It can bear joy, sorrow, pain up to a certain point, but perishes as soon as this threshold is exceeded. Thus it is not a question as to whether one is weak or strong, but as to whether one can endure the measure of one's own suffering, be it moral or physical. I find it just as peculiar to say that the man who takes his life is a coward, as it would be inappropriate to call another a coward for dying of a virulent fever."[18] At the end of the novel, like some hero of medical history, poor Werther falls victim to the disease on which he has become so expert. He has long argued that an understanding of suicide is of no help in preventing one's own. When snubbed by the nobility at the court where he is engaged, he resigns and returns to his Lotte, who is married by now. Here he succumbs to introspection, depression, and Jerusalem's death.

According to some very late autobiographical jottings, *Werther* became the topic for discussion between its author and Napoleon when they met in 1808. It was presumably on this occasion that the emperor claimed he had taken the little novel along with him on his Egyptian campaign. He praised the work while at the same time demonstrating his critical acumen by remarking how, since it is a love story, the episode in which Werther is socially snubbed by the nobility constitutes a flaw in artistic form. At fifty-nine, Goethe appears to have been courtier enough to agree with Napoleon, and perhaps the issue was no longer of great consequence to him.[19] Yet to a twenty-four-year-old middle-class poet the perception of Jerusalem's social embarrassment as analogous to the loss of feminine love and appreciation was crucial to his novel. Both, he was sure, can debase a young man's self-esteem and even his sense of identity. The news of Jerusalem's death in Wetzlar, coming as it did right after his own summer there and on the heels of Cornelia's engagement, meant that warp and woof of Goethe's first great work had been provided.

Still, he was long unsure how to go about handling them. He spent a year and more casting around for the proper form, apparently during this period never doubting that his was an exclusively dramatic talent. The epistolary novel (consisting of letters exchanged among two or more characters) had been cultivated throughout the century, and Goethe's matronly friend Sophie de la Roche had brought it to a peak of popularity in Germany. Goethe was to follow her lead in letting one individual write all the letters, something especially convenient for a youth who had for years already been practicing a kind of epistolary narrative of his own life. Throughout 1773, however, he was preoccupied with dramatic efforts.

The revision of *Götz* in the spring of this year had led to very satisfactory results. "When I published my *Götz*, it was one of my sweetest hopes that my friends, of whom I do have quite a few in the world, would be reminded of me and perhaps think of me in a more pleasant sense than some long, insignificant correspondence might accomplish. And that is what has happened. Your letter . . . was extraordinarily satisfying for me."[20] Although *Götz* had been well enough received on a small scale in the 1771 manuscript, the unprecedented popular response to its printing was overwhelming for the young writer. Since he had what he called a "natural bent" to dramatize everything, we are not surprised at his threat, made already in April, 1773, "to cast a most accurate likeness" of the Kestners (Lotte was married by now) onto the stage.[21] As the general success of *Götz* became apparent, Goethe hurled himself into all sorts of new dramatic plans, but none was very successful, and most of them remained fragments. One was the Wetzlar-Jerusalem subject, about which he was serious enough to warn the Kestners in advance: "I am keeping busy, and if I have good luck you'll soon get something more in a new style. I wish Lotte weren't indifferent toward my drama [*Götz*]. It has brought me all kinds of laudatory wreaths made of all varieties of greenery and flowers, even Italian ones. I have tried each of them on and laughed at myself in the mirror. . . . A year ago today things were different, and I would swear that at this moment I was sitting with Lotte. Come hell or high water I am going to make a play out of my situation. I know what Lotte will say when she sees it, and I know what my answer will be."[22] The "new style" which he recognized as necessary could not be developed — not, at any rate, for a drama. The fragments of dramas from 1773 are in the same archaic language of *Götz* and often in the Hans Sachs tone which favored irony, that sole redeemer of Goethe's heavy youthful pathos. *Faust I* contains the best-known example of this style.

The whole point with the Wetzlar subject was to achieve full sympathy with Jerusalem's point of view, which Goethe was finally to present with the same eloquence as he had the political views of Götz. Werther cries out, for example: "Oh you reasonable people. . . . Passion! Drunkenness! Madness! You stand by so complacent, so devoid of sympathy, you moral people! Scold the drinker! Despise the madman! Walk past on the other side like the priest and thank God like the Pharisee that He has not made you like one of these. I have been drunk more than once; my own passions were never far from madness, and I regret neither."[23] It is Werther's argument that "we can discuss a man's case, with honor, only in so far as we share his feelings." This purpose of presenting various points of view sympathetically seemed to Goethe at the time to be a dramatic one. He accompanied Werther along the path to madness just far enough to contemplate the drama's end, but he was able to do so in a purposeful kind of detachment. To be sure, fear of losing his own identity among the great mass was an almost pathological fear in Goethe's own heart. In Werther he allowed it to develop a psychotic course. For his own part he hoped to call up sufficient resolve, perseverance, and technical cunning to employ this same anxiety in constructing a world of fancy. In this way he hoped again to speak to the hearts of his contemporaries as he had, with *Götz,* proved he could.

Scholars have speculated about what at last brought the *Werther* material to congeal in the spring of 1774. One popular notion is that the marriage to a Frankfurt merchant of one of Madame de la Roche's daughters, of whom Goethe was very fond, produced in him an emotional state which found release in writing. While it is entirely true that his writing had a therapeutic value for him, it would be a considerable oversimplification to suppose that he could overcome his frustrations by writing a book, poem, or play on the subject. One of our main purposes will be to look into the importance of Goethe's writing for his long-term personality problems. Here it is enough to observe that, insofar as emotional crises can be directly related to his poetic output, a significant time lapse usually separates the personal problem from the work connected with it.

In 1774 he was in fact troubled not by one marriage, but by what appeared to be the pairing off of just about all the friends of his youth. Would he, too, become a good Frankfurt husband? Neither this prospect nor that of remaining a bachelor seemed very attractive. His professional future also looked like a choice among evils. His response when Kestner offered to arrange for his appointment at the Hanover court gives us an idea of his thinking in this regard: "It is true that my father would have nothing against my entering into the service of another land, and since neither love nor expectation of office holds me here it seems I could make the try and see how things are over there. On the other hand, Kestner, I want to put my talents and potential to my own personal use. I have always been accustomed to act only in accordance with my own urges, and that is no way to serve a prince. I would be a long time learning subordination, too."[24] It is possible that he appreciated now for the first time just how damaging it might be to his self-esteem if he, like Jerusalem, were exposed to a court environment and its caste system. It may be that it was not until Kestner's offer that he saw the connection between this aspect of Jerusalem's experience and Jerusalem's ill-starred love affair. Goethe's first reference to *Werther* as a novel might lead us to think this is the case. In the middle of February, 1774, he mentions to Sophie de la Roche a work "which I began after you left, really began, because I never had the idea of making one individual whole out of this topic."

That important trait which Goethe shared with his Werther, an urgent need to prove his own uniqueness among the vast namelessness of the mass, provided the force which synthesized his experiences with those of Jerusalem in an extremely intimate autobiographical novel. Kestner, Lotte, her father and brothers and sisters are all in it, so that contemporaries as well as posterity have been able to seek out a wealth of parallels. There are many differences, too. What interests us is that Goethe must have been closely acquainted with Werther's emotional state, and we must infer a very similar crisis on his part. Werther's self-esteem had been undermined both in his career and in his private life. Goethe knew the same anxiety, but as a result of his new novel he became a celebrity.

We probably have to make a special effort in our times to imagine the excited attention which the eighteenth century accorded its poets. The first to enjoy great numbers of fans was Klopstock, whose odes to his sweetheart had evoked strong participation from the young at mid-century. He tested the winds on a trip through Germany in the spring of 1775 by pretending, when in a small town "where they don't read at all," that his traveling companion was Goethe. The result was a great sensation among the villagers, who accorded the companion such "great respect" as to ignore Klopstock himself.[25] A sampling of letters out of the summer of 1775 may help form an idea of the atmosphere in Germany just before Goethe went to Weimar.

A prominent critic of the older generation speaks with due reserve: "This young scholar is a true *Originalgenie,* quite free in his thinking on political as well as scholarly topics. While possessed of sharp judgment, fiery imagination, and lively sensitivity, his opinions about people, customs, politics, and taste are as yet unsupported by sufficient experience. I found his company pleasant and engaging."[26]

A more typical passage from a young traveler: "He is one of the leading authors in Germany and belongs to that group who are beginning to start a new sect. The very least that they propose is the abolition of all rules set up for the theater by Boileau, du Bos, Marmontel, Voltaire, etc., and the establishment of

Shakespeare as the sole model worthy of emulation. He is also the author of *Gods Heroes and Wieland*. . . . Wieland, whom all the world once feared, now trembles before him."[27]

A letter written after Goethe called: "If I had but been permitted a single hour more to see, hear, enjoy this man! From the hair of his head down to his footprint, in every vein, feature, movement, you recognize that he is the man who could write *Werther*. He left a handkerchief here, but I am not capable of returning it to him. This remembrance of his existence will remain with me."[28]

"Actually, in his writings he is an actor, in his life a wild fellow, and an artist, and a good boy," commented a man who knew him well, his friend Herder.[29] Yet to the world Goethe had become a celebrity, visited by all the cultured who passed through Frankfurt. "At first it looks very elegant, and you think you are in the house of a minister of state. His reception, or audience room is never empty, one new visitor constantly replacing the last. Goethe really is inconvenienced, because every traveler wants to make his acquaintance. Now, however, he gives audience only four times a week in the morning. The rest of the time goes to his friends and to his affairs."[30]

NOTES

1. December 23, 1774.
2. To Charlotte on June 16 and July 9, 1786.
3. To Carl August on December 12, 1786.
4. July 24, 1786.
5. To Charlotte on June 25, 1786.
6. To August von Hennings in November. Bode, 33 ff. Kestner is not being malicious about the question of Goethe's doctorate. Goethe did indeed use the title when young. He felt he had reason to consider his French diploma as the equivalent.
7. October 8, 1772.
8. To Kestner on October 27, 1772.
9. Werther's letter of August 28, 1771 (Goethe's birthday). *JA* 16, 60 f.
10. November, 1772.

Questions about Individuality

11. *Dichtung und Wahrheit, Buch VI. JA* 23, 16.
12. October 10, 1772.
13. Early November, 1772.
14. To Kestner on November 10, 1772.
15. To Sophie de la Roche, about November 20, 1772.
16. November 29, 1772.
17. Werther's letter of May 22, 1771. *JA* 16, 12.
18. Werther's letter of August 12, 1771.
19. Or perhaps Goethe recognized that Napoleon, coached for the meeting, was not expressing his own views. See *Unterredung mit Napoleon,* 1808. *JA* 30, 411-416.
20. To Langer, October, 1773.
21. To Kestner on April 14, 1773.
22. To Kestner in July, 1773.
23. Werther's letter of August 12, 1771. *JA* 16, 51.
24. December 25, 1773.
25. Boie to Merck on April 10, 1775. In Heinz Amelung, *Goethe als Persönlichkeit,* 1 (Munich, 1914), 113.
26. Johann Georg Sulzer's *Tagebuch.* Grumach 1, 366.
27. Iselin to Frey on April 27, 1775. Bode, 126.
28. Hotze to Lavater on July 2, 1775. Herwig, 149-50.
29. July, 1775. Bode, 138.
30. Götz to his parents on September 30, 1775. Grumach 1, 368.

Hohe Minne

$$\text{✦}$$

Man's feelings toward women are charged with ambivalence, and each culture has to come to terms with the consequences as best it can. The middle-class Protestant ethos in which Goethe grew up may indeed have been more productive of conflicts in this sector than of their satisfactory resolution. While the man who associates sex with guilt and frustration may feel torn between dionysiac urges and his desire to revere the undefiled, courtly society seems in its best moments to have provided clear forms for separating the two. A man might idealize his mistress in a way which he could claim to be as pure as his devotion to sister, mother, or Holy Virgin. In the Middle Ages this was called *Hohe Minne*. Sexuality could be relegated to an entirely different social realm — girls of the village, perhaps a wife from his own social stratum — while the mistress stood at the remove of a higher estate, was perhaps even wed to his liege lord.

When young, Goethe shared with many sensitive boys that strong hesitation to recognize sexuality as coloring his feelings toward the beloved; he was probably quite confident that no such emotions affected his attachment to Cornelia. After their relationship was terminated abruptly by her marriage and departure from Frankfurt in early 1773, he continued to cherish it as a kind of ideal love. Hence it is understandable if in his first weeks in Weimar he felt himself drawn to two women who were of his sister's slender frame and aloofness, even coldness, toward men. The most scanty and indirect documentation of one of these associations, his homage to Carl August's young bride, survives; the other, with her lady-in-waiting Charlotte von Stein, produced a twelve-year correspondence so prolific and so filled with secrets that it sometimes seems to have cast the entire body of Goethe biography out of balance. He himself often compared the relationship to his love for his sister; in any case, it was one of those sentimental attachments possible, perhaps even comprehensible, only in the still courtly atmosphere of the rococo.

The Lady Charlotte celebrated her thirty-third birthday the Christmas after Goethe arrived in Weimar; the Duchess Louise had her nineteenth a month later. It was a difference in ages which seemed greater then than now, and it probably obscured Goethe's perception of a similarity in temperament and circumstance between the two women which, over the years, was to form the basis for their own close friendship. Both were sensitive, delicate women, the younger destined to suffer from inconsiderate treatment by a more lusty husband, Charlotte now at the end of a long period of similar suffering — after her seventh child her physician had arranged that she refrain from having more. Even their men had much in common; Carl August was a great lover of dogs, with which he overran Louise's court, and the Lord Josias von Stein served as his marshal of the hunt.

The lot of womankind was harsher in those days: marriage their only option in life, but love often overshadowed by a justified horror of childbirth, midwifery still in an unbelievably superstitious stage. The poet in Goethe felt a tender interest and need to encompass feminine experience and woman's outlook. He had naturally been influenced by his sympathy for an utterly frigid and frightened sister, whose uncertain health was in these very years being undermined by a regular sequence of childbirths.

67

What wonder that women like Louise and Charlotte both attracted and welcomed his interest? How eagerly they must have greeted a presence which seemed to ennoble their difficult lot and to encourage their private fancy! Both were flattered by the highly sentimentalized devotion of their poet during his first ebullient months at court, and he was very conscious of the kind of appeal he had for them — the Lady Charlotte, at any rate, reproached him for being too much the coquette (a word at that time applicable to young dandies).[1] With time, homage to his duchess became the solicitous attention of an old friend of the family. The relationship with Charlotte von Stein, on the other hand, developed over the next few years into an extremely late and surely the most stunning flower in the historical garden of courtly love.

Many writers have sought to capture its rare beauty; indeed, several interpretations have themselves taken artistic form. Here we shall be satisfied with a brief overview of some of Goethe's letters to the Lady. Literally thousands of *billets-doux* must have been exchanged between his coming to Weimar in 1775 and his return from Italy in 1788. We have scores of inquiries as to how she slept, what mood she is in, how her foot is (she suffered slightly from the gout); there survive endless little slips of paper which accompanied asparagus or strawberries from his garden; there are thoughtful discussions of the difficulties in the ducal family, and there are lengthy travel diaries, but the correspondence is characterized by the outpouring of Goethe's own intimate personal confessions. The remarkable openness of these letters renders them one of our very best sources for tracing his attitudes on a wide range of subjects. Her records, on the other hand, are closed. She requested the return of her own letters and, presumably, destroyed them.

Here are some excerpts from his, typical of the first months:

1776, February: "You have my full confidence and, if God be

willing, I will in time confide fully in you. Oh, if my sister had a brother like I have a sister in you!"

April: "Adieu dear sister, if sister it must be. Do you have the feeling that you will see me today? Here is something for the monkeys [her sons]. If you feel like it, make me a copy of my poem. I don't have one now, and I would like to have it from your hand — then I will let you alone."

May: "Good morning! Yesterday, dear Lady, I had difficulty keeping my vow, and I shall have difficulty with your command today, too. Since my love for you is a continuous self-denial, however, let it be. Remember me."

A fortnight later: "Here a letter from my sister. You will understand how it tears at my heart. I kept a few letters to myself before this one, so as not to trouble you. I urgently beg you to be her friend, write to her, plague me until I send her some word. Farewell."

Still in May: "Now this relationship, too, the purest, loveliest, truest that I ever had with a woman other than my sister, it, too, is darkened. . . . I will not come to see you. Seeing you would make me sad. If I am not to live with you, then your love can help me just as little as does that of those far away, of whom I have so many. Presence in the moment of need is all-important, all-soothing, all-strengthening. The absent friend comes too late and brings his fire pump to a house that is already burned out. — And all this for the sake of people's opinion. The opinions of those who mean nothing to me, and who do not want you to mean anything to me, either. They know not what they do. One who is shut up in solitude, deaf to the voice of love, can easily do others hurt. Adieu, my best one."

August: "Your relationship to me is so sacredly unique that I have only now come to sense clearly how it can neither be expressed in words nor seen by man. Perhaps it will soothe me for a few moments to turn my past sufferings to a drama again."

We can probably assume that the Lady gave little encouragement to the extravagant emotionality of this wooing in its first year. Her thinking was somewhat conventional and very strongly oriented toward her religion. That in this, too, she was attractive to Goethe is apparent from the close of a note to her as she left for her country estate in October: "For a time now you have seemed to me like a Madonna ascending into Heaven, in vain that one remaining behind stretches forth his arms after her, in vain that his tearful farewell gaze calls her back just once more — she is lost in the aura that surrounds her, full of longing only for the crown that awaits her above. Farewell. I do love you." On the back of this same sheet the Lady Charlotte indited a poem in awkward Alexandrian lines and half-lines which constitutes her first and most extensive surviving response — not a reply, for he never received it — to Goethe's love:

> Be it a crime to feel my longing,
> And if the soul must penance do for heart's sweet wronging?
> — To answer, conscience does refuse me.
> Destroy it, Heaven! if it ever could accuse me.

A letter from the next year bears, after his "Adieu, best one," her penciled: "Adieu, adieu!"[2]

In the summer of 1777 Goethe suffered the terrific blow of his sister's death. He had little understanding for the exigencies of a house full of little children, so her widower's remarriage within a few months added to his grief. Now his devotion to the Lady Charlotte becomes his sole emotional attachment of any significance at all, and his letters increase in poetic depth. In November he wonders "whether I really love you or only delight in being near you, as before a glass so pure that I can see myself clearly in it." Her increasing sway over him becomes apparent from the religious overtones which their relationship is acquiring: "To know that you are on the way here is my whole desire, and

that you might love me and like me to know that you do. For
faith lives on the heavenly manna of sacraments."[3]

We often get the impression that his devotion has itself taken
on a kind of ritual character: "My soul has attached itself firmly
to yours, I do not care to talk about it, you know that I am inseparable from you and that neither high nor low can take me
away. I wish that there were some kind of vow or sacrament
which would visibly and legally make me yours, how I would
treasure it! My novitiate has, after all, given me time enough
to consider it. . . . The Jews have cords with which they entwine
their arms when praying, and so I wind your dear ribbon around
my arm when I say my prayers to you and beg that I may partake of your goodness, wisdom and patience."[4] This is from the
spring of 1781, a time when his letters became, for about a year,
particularly intense. It is interesting to observe that this period
also constitutes an important node of creativity in Goethe's life —
virtually all the works which we are considering in this biography
were conceived or written or revised in the years around 1781 —
while his most ardent and dedicated administrative efforts also
reached a peak at this time.

Perhaps it was in the spring of 1782 that the Lady at last confessed her own love to him. "Oh my best one! My whole life long
I have had an idealistic dream of how I would like to be loved,
and in vain have sought fulfillment in fanciful visions. Now, with
the world lying daily clearer out before me, I find it at last in
you and in a form which can never perish. A thousand farewells."[5] On the eve of a trip in April he writes: "Good night
Lotte. Fare you well dear certainty, dearest dream of my life."
And while away: "How different everything looks now that I
know what love awaits me beyond the mountains."

What kind of woman was the partner in this famous love?
We know almost nothing about her during the period in ques-

tion. The most objective statements were made by Friedrich Schiller, but he did not meet her until the time of Goethe's absence in Italy, when she was forty-four. His first impression was, "she can never have been beautiful, but her face does have a gentle seriousness and a quite unique candor." As he came to know her better, he admitted that he would like to be with her daily: "I feel comfortable in her presence."[6] If we wish any intimation from her own pen as to how she felt about Goethe, we have to turn to an even later period, when the Lady in her fifties wrote to her son about love: "I am incapable of instinctual love, as I observe it in many. I require perfection, insofar as this is possible here below, in the object which I find attractive." Or again: "Lasting love can be maintained, I think, only by the mutual striving to become a better person for the sake of the other."[7] A relationship of this sort asked that both parties examine their psychic condition with great honesty. It is as a consequence of such delving on Goethe's part that we have, from the spring of 1779, the drama *Iphigenia*.[8]

The heroine is that daughter whom Agamemnon sacrificed for favorable winds to sail against Troy. Diana substituted a faun on the altar, so as to spirit the victim away alive to her temple in Tauris. During the ten-year seige of Troy, Agamemnon's wife entered an adulterous relationship which culminated in his murder when he returned. A banished son, Orestes, too young to avenge his father immediately, returned as a man to slay both his mother and her lover. Goethe's drama opens with Orestes' arrival in Tauris, driven to madness by ancient avenging spirits, the Furies. His sister, now in her thirties, has remained Diana's priestess, a "holy virgin," her "innermost thought still enshrouded in bitter secrecy" despite the gentle wooing of the benevolent king of Tauris. To her, his courtship seems a "most terrible threat," and when pressed as to why she feels this way, she explains: "This is why my wounded heart cannot heal. In my early youth, just when my soul was attaching itself to father, mother, brother, and sister, just when the new sprouts at the feet of the old trees were striving toward heaven in their sweet company, I became enmeshed in the misery of my family, was saved by divine benevolence and brought here by a miracle — such deep scars now remain in my breast from those old injuries that neither joy nor hope can thrive there." The only complaint of the mythological Iphigenia had been precisely that sacrifice which Goethe's Iphigenia welcomes as having released her from the misery of her family when she was a child. Those old injuries and scars are now made responsible for her anxiety at the approach of the king, and for her repeated deploring of woman's condition. It is astonishing how sympathetically, in what an entirely positive light Goethe succeeds in presenting this virginal personality to us, repelled as she is by masculinity and dissatisfied with femininity.

Naturally opposed to all that is carnal, she has used her office as priestess of Diana to abolish traditional Taurian blood sacrifices of strangers. The king, piqued that Iphigenia continues to spurn him, now decrees reinstatement of the old rites. The two unidentified Greeks, Orestes and his friend Pylades, shall be the first victims. Like Iphigenia, Orestes tells us of early scars: "The dark cowl of life lay about my tender head from childhood on. Subject to a mother who forgot her absent spouse, I grew up oppressed, in my innocence a bitter reproach to her and to her lover." Now, as matricide, he is in mental turmoil, and the crux of the drama is the therapy he finds in the custody of his unrecognized sister.

It begins when he must render her an account of the Trojan War, of Agamemnon's return and murder, and at last of his own deed, as if he were telling of someone else's family. "Thus the gods have chosen me as herald of the deed which I should wish to hide in those barren, silent caverns of ancient night. I am compelled against my will to speak, for your sweet mouth can ask, even require what is painful, and be obeyed." From the outset he feels such complete confidence in the strange priestess that he can conceal nothing from her — not even, finally, who he is: "Let there be, between us, truth."

Iphigenia prays to Diana for help, then asks Orestes if he cannot remember two sisters from his early childhood. "I can remember only one. A good turn of fate removed the other from the misery of our house early. — Oh, cease your questioning. Do not join those Furies who eternally blow the ash from my heart and will not let the final coal die, the burning horror of our family. Must the red glow of guilt be fanned eternally, fed with the sulfur of hell, to burn in my soul?" Orestes' mind turns inward and back toward precisely those past circumstances and actions of his which have undermined his sanity. He feels animosity toward the woman who has forced these memories on him, and lashes out at her: "Your terrible voice strikes to the innermost depths of my mind." He even accuses her of sexual interest in him, "wanton, forbidden lust," but at last he becomes aware of the companion of his early years: "Since my childhood years I have loved nothing as I was able to love you, sister." He faints, exhausted. A dream reveals his parents reconciled, even his ancestors on good terms, except for one whom he is forbidden to see, poor tortured Tantalus, father of the long line of transgressors and sufferers.

Two elements are stressed in Orestes' "cure," or release from the Furies. His consciousness is forced, despite great resistance, to open itself to the past. He faces these unsettling visions under the gentle compulsion and with the support of his sister. Human-to-human contact seems to have been decisive from Goethe's point of view. One sibling finds he can help the other on the way to honesty with himself about himself or, as he called it in a later comment, on the way to "pure humanity."

Striving for ultimate honesty is also the topic of an ongoing discussion between Orestes and his friend Pylades. The introspection of the hero contrasts with Pylades' eagerness to come to grips with the outer world. Goethe characteristically used two main characters to present fundamental contradictions with which most of us must come to terms as individuals. Here the active life of accomplishment and attendant guilt (Pylades) is juxtaposed with a reflective life devoted to truth. Orestes' healing, as the high point of the drama, makes honesty appear to be an essential underpinning of sanity. Still, the problem remains as to how the escape from Tauris shall be effected. Pylades argues that the only practical hope is to deceive the king. Iphigenia must lie to him.

She becomes involved in a difficult argument on this score. Pylades insists that saving her brother's life is a noble end which justifies dishonest means; she, that "only the utterly unblemished know peace of mind." Pylades observes: "In the temple you have found it possible to be unblemished. In the eyes of men, the merely partially blemished pass for clean. . . . Nor are we supposed to pass judgment on ourselves. Man is meant to keep his eye on the road ahead, for seldom does he judge past deeds rightly, and present actions almost never." Iphigenia: "Then he acts well who inquires of his soul." The drama fixes and holds its focus on the necessity of honesty with ourselves.

Many have "identified" Iphigenia with Charlotte, but she incorporates features which remind us of Cornelia, too, and also of Goethe himself. When we consider the work as a whole, we have the impression that it does point up that distinctive and eternally fascinating quality of Goethe's and Charlotte's love: mystical idealization combined with great depth of psychological understanding. His letters to her include dozens of notes like the following: "Tell me dear Lotte, how did you feel when you got up? Tell me, is it physical or is there something in your mind that is painful to you? The sole interest of my life is that you will be open with me. I cannot endure anything that is closed up in it-

75

self."[9] He urges her to be surer of her own worth, less fearful, brooding, and superstitious, not to place so much stock in her dreams and — over and over again — to be more open with him, to express her fears and frustrations. We are startled by his psychological finesse in detailing to her the plight of the Duchess of Meiningen: "If she could just find some object to elicit her affection, then, with luck, she might have something to look forward to. As for the countess, she is certainly attractive and capable of interesting and keeping a man. The duchess is, too, but in her case the bud, if I may express it thus, never opens. One who is closed closes all others, just as he who is open opens them, expecially when both are of a higher nature."[10]

He seems to have felt that one of the greatest benefits he could offer a woman like Charlotte was his own need for her help. "At your feet I beg you, complete your work, make me very good. You can do so, not just by loving me — your power is infinitely increased by your faith that I love you."[11] In this way archaic courtly love merged with modern psychotherapy. Their relationship was characterized by the lady's educative influence on her admirer, from mere superficialities in the early years when Goethe was uncertain of court etiquette, to the more difficult questions which he soon faced, such as how to maintain a serene mental state in the face of administrative, political, and other worldly strife. His need for her was by no means counterfeited. He was a highly volatile individual, often inclined in the direction which a modern clinician calls manic depressive. The real benefit which he drew from the relationship was one for which she may not have been consciously responsible at first. In her service he found an emotional stability which he had never known before, even when at home with Cornelia. At the high point of his *Minnedienst* the lady surely did understand this, however; he certainly told her often enough:

I am happy because in the midst of multifarious, strange humanity I find my way by the thread of love to you, softly and securely. As the mussels swim when they open their bodies out of their shell, I too learn to live by gently opening out what is closed within me. I am testing all the things we discussed recently about behavior, bearing, dignity, and noblesse. I am relaxed, yet always attentive to what I am doing. I can assure you that all whom I observe are playing a role to a far greater extent than I. How pleasant this game becomes for me when I have no other purpose or wish than to please you and to be welcomed back! You shall partake of my entire harvest when I return.[12]

Unfortunately, the lady had scarcely revealed to Goethe that she returned his love before she began making demands on his "fidelity" which he found a little amusing. When visiting a friend well known for her beauty, he remarks that it is no doubt the Lady Charlotte's jealousy that sent the bad weather.[13] Occasionally he is even moved to address a gentle reproach to her. His official duties and especially attendance at neighboring courts entailed associations with highly cultivated, sometimes both beautiful and flirtatious noblewomen who thought him fascinating. He found in their ways of thinking and in their sensibilities a valuable complement to his own realms and modes of experience. No other poet has ever been able to display such depth of sympathy for specifically feminine traits and feelings. His reaction to Charlotte's quibbling was always in good humor, and he usually yielded to her wishes.

As he became more and more frustrated in his official life but found at the same time a less and less satisfactory release in drawing and writing, she was his mainstay. Unfortunately, Charlotte was herself approaching an irritable time of life in her mid-forties, so that his letters include more and more notes like the following: "Since it appears that we cannot talk to each other I will take my leave in writing, lest we become utter strangers."[14] By the year of the Italian trip this love, which had evoked some of his most touching lyrics, was an extremely important element in his personal development; but it seemed to constitute an epoch now, valued more for its past than for its present effectiveness. "Do, my love, whatever and however you see fit, and it will suit me, too. Continue to love me, and let us at least hold on to what we shall never find again, even if there are moments when we are unable to enjoy it."[15]

A strong bond between Charlotte and Goethe existed in her youngest son, Fritz.* One winter morning in 1778 the five-year-old had undertaken the long walk from his own house up the river to Goethe's cottage, bringing him breakfast. This became a frequent trip for him as the weather improved, and by March he was being sent back home with flowers and fruits for his mother. Often he spent the night with Goethe, and before the year was out this, too, had become a habit. The man had a special weakness for children and a strong paternal urge. He had already assumed one legal guardianship, that of a Swiss boy, Peter im Baumgarten, whose foster father had died in the American Revolution. Peter had been put in the care of the tutor to the von Stein boys and sent to their country home. He turned out to be a really difficult child and a disappointment in many ways. Fritz was an entirely different experience, bright, responsive, and affectionate. Charlotte was not a mother who liked to spend a lot of time with children, and Goethe eagerly assumed complete responsibility for her youngest. He especially liked to take Fritz on trips with him, not just to Ilmenau and other nearby towns. When he was nine they went to Dessau and Leipzig; when he was ten, on a month's excursion into the Harz Mountains, and back there again in the next year. In 1783, after several years of close association, Fritz actually moved into Goethe's house and lived there until after Goethe's departure for Italy. Goethe looked

78

after his education, took the boy along on inspection trips, on formal calls at neighboring courts, and to his office, where the two read and discussed the merits of petitions received by the Lord Privy Councilor and President of the Chamber. One of the most unaccustomed circumstances of the trip to Italy in 1786 was Fritz's absence.

While still in Carlsbad that summer Goethe began admonishing his secretary Seidel not to write without sending some word of Fritz,[16] and his final instructions before departing included provision for Fritz to continue living at his house.[17] Already from Regensburg there is a note in his diary: "I wish I had brought Fritz, after all."[18] The first of the really lovely Italian cities, Verona, with its many new impressions, makes him sad that the child is not there: "Had I known what I know now, I would have brought him, after all."[19] In Venice he wished Fritz with him "a hundred times," and remarked, touchingly, that he was looking forward to seeing him.[20] As soon as he arrived in Rome, he sent word to Fritz that he was sorry not to have him along and that he was making a lot of collections for him.[21] The boy, now fourteen, held out faithfully in Goethe's house for four months, although he had had no word whatever from his friend. At last, in December, he took his things back to his mother's place, and she told Goethe so. "It saddens me to hear that Fritz is no longer in my house," Goethe replied. "I thought I had done the right thing. I had put him in my room and arranged for Seidel to sleep with him — Let this be the last time, God help me, that I go through with an undertaking of this sort in silence. May some good genius always touch my lips and open them."[22]

The departure for Italy had actually meant no interruption in the steady stream of writing for the Lady Charlotte. Goethe's need to communicate his feelings to someone appreciative of him led, just as in the *Werther* epoch, to a kind of compulsive letter-writing. The urge was naturally strongest when he was loneliest;

hence his diary for Charlotte is continuous and extensive during the first few weeks away. It is characteristic of him that, once the need to communicate with his loved ones had been met by writing, he felt then no strong call actually to mail any letters. He wanted to keep his whereabouts and destination secret for a time, and it appears never to have occurred to him that the Lady would be distressed by a lengthy silence. He posted the diary when he left Venice in mid-October — or so he reported — but she did not receive the package until after the first of the year. That is to say, in an era when travel was exceptional and dangerous, Charlotte remained ignorant of his safety for about three months. Nor did he show any real sympathy when she complained bitterly[23] — and this was not typical of Goethe, for he was usually an understanding kind of friend. The Lady Charlotte must have become ever more of an ideal for him, particularly at this geographical remove, and less the flesh-and-blood woman whose feelings had once been the object of his concern.

Although it is true that his letters and diaries are more intimate than any in German before him, and that the materials for Charlotte rise frequently to an extraordinary degree of expressiveness, still they do not vie with his poetic writing in adequacy and efficiency of expression. Werther's letters to his friend, for example, were specifically conceived as a higher kind of communication, as Goethe said, "with the best souls of my era." When he came to revise that novel, it turned out to be a wonderful channel of communication with himself, too, into his own past. The same is probably true of *Iphigenia*. He had the manuscript with him on his way to Venice, and he worked on it during his brief stay there. In Bologna he "found a Saint Agatha by Raphael which, although damaged, is a precious image. He gave her a sure virginity, without charm, but without coldness or harshness. I noted it well and shall hold this ideal up to my *Iphigenia*. I shall allow my heroine to say nothing which this saint might not have said."[24] In Rome *Iphigenia* became his first project, a considerably more thorough revision than that of *Werther,* because the prose was being transformed to iambic pentameter.

By the middle of January he was able to send it off to Herder. He certainly did so with the hope that it would soften Charlotte's hard feelings toward him and encourage others to think well of him, too. Herder was asked to read the revision closely against the original and make whatever corrections seemed necessary to assure euphony — this despite the new metrics, which he claimed were based on important insights gained in Italy. We cannot help inferring that one of his major concerns, even if an unconscious one, must have been that they remember him at home by reading his works attentively and sympathetically. "Take it now, and may it profit from your kind efforts. Read it with the women; let the Lady Charlotte see it; you and your wife give your blessings to her reading of it. . . . I am myself a troubled stranger in the land. Visions are showered on me not by the Furies, but by the Muses and Graces and the whole power of the blessed gods."

The major goal in rewriting was to work toward an idealized form for *Iphigenia* to correspond with the ideal perception it conveys. Changing the prose to verse was an important part of the job. Goethe wanted to handle the meter in a way similar to the ancients' construction of their amphitheaters, temples, and aqueducts. The perfect regularity of form would be at the same time functional, in that only those syllables which carried the burden of meaning would be permitted metric stress. What was involved, then, was a careful reconsideration of every word, a much deeper reworking than the final redaction of *Werther.* Still, while he hoped that the Italian sky would be apparent to the readers of *Iphigenia,* he did not intend any fundamental change in the original conception. At times he even succeeded in making it more explicit. Nowhere, for example, had the rivalry between

Orestes and the king within Iphigenia's heart come through so clearly as in the lines given her in Rome:

> A wheel of joy and pain turns through my soul.
> A shudder thrusts me from this alien man,
> And yet so forcefully I'm drawn unto
> My brother.

Certain minor changes are interesting for quite a different reason. The original seems to have retained too clear an imprint from personal experience not consonant with the dramatic action. We noted, for example, Iphigenia's remembrance of early scars on her personality when "enmeshed in the misery of my family," and how she was grateful for the sacrifice which released her. The Italian revision goes back to the traditional situation,

> An alien curse that seized and parted me
> From those I loved.

A similar, subtle rewording occurs in Orestes' case. These are small matters, yet they may be clues to the channels taken by creative springs.

It was Goethe's wont to think over in the evening the writing he would undertake the next day, sleep on it, then use the early morning hours for work. His lodging in Rome was with a painter, Wilhelm Tischbein. Tischbein wrote to a mutual friend in Switzerland:

> What I like so much about Goethe is his simple life. He desired of me a little room where he could sleep and work undisturbed, and extremely simple food. I was able to give him both very easily, because it takes so little to satisfy him. Now he sits in there and works mornings until nine at finishing his *Iphigenia*. He goes out then and looks at the great works of art here. You can easily imagine the eye and the knowledge with which he fastens upon them, because you know how genuine his thinking is. He refuses to be disturbed very much by the prominent people, makes no visits and accepts none except from artists. There

was the plan of honoring him in the same way other great poets who have been in Rome before were honored. He excused himself, however, on account of the time which would be consumed, thus in a courteous manner avoiding the appearance of vanity. It certainly does him just as much honor as being crowned with laurel at the Capitoline Hill.[25]

About the same time Goethe wrote to Charlotte:

I read my *Iphigenia* to Tischbein. It is almost finished. I was startled by the strange, original manner with which he regarded the piece and explained to me the condition in which I had conceived it. Words cannot express how sharply and deeply he sensed the human being behind the heroic mask. — When you also consider that I am compelled to look at my other works and to contemplate how I intend to conclude them and arrange them, and that I am required by this activity to enter again into a thousand past situations in my life, and that all this is crowding in upon me in the most remarkable city in the world, which would by itself be enough to confuse a new arrival, then you can imagine my frame of mind.[26]

NOTES

1. Charlotte to Zimmermann on March 8, 1776. Bode, 175 f.
2. See the notes to the Weimar ed. of letters nos. 519 and 611.
3. May 30, 1779.
4. March 12, 1781.
5. March 20, 1782.
6. To Körner on August 12, 1787. *Schillers Briefwechsel mit Körner* (Leipzig, 1878), I, 136.
7. Quoted by Wilhelm Bode, *Charlotte von Stein* (Berlin, 1910), p. 430.
8. My translations are from the 1779, or prose version of *Iphigenia*.
9. July 19, 1782.
10. April 12, 1782.
11. March 12, 1781.
12. March 31, 1782.
13. Marie Antonie de Branconi on September 9-10, 1783. In Flodoard Freiherr von Biedermann, *Goethes Gespräche* (Leipzig, 1909–), I, 118.
14. August 31, 1785.

15. June 25, 1786.
16. On August 13, 1786, for example.
17. To Seidel on September 2, 1786. Also to Fritz on the same day.
18. September 5, 1786.
19. Diary for Charlotte, September 18, 1786.
20. Ibid., October 14, 1786.
21. To Charlotte on December 2, 1786.
22. To Charlotte on December 29, 1786.
23. January 13, 1787.
24. *Italienische Reise,* October 19, 1786.
25. Tischbein to Lavater, December 9, 1786. Bode, 341.
26. December 14, 1786.

Political Engagement

THE younger von Kalb succeeded his father as President of the Chamber in 1776, in the same summer in which Goethe received his own first appointment. Both young men had high hopes of bettering the condition of the duchy by reducing the tax burdens and rationalizing the economy — hopes which drew their main nourishment from youthful good will and ignorance of the circumstances. The administration of Weimar was already honest and, compared with neighboring principalities, as efficient as might be expected. The feudal order of things was hopelessly unjust, but it was also hopelessly entrenched. Any significant progress would have required replacement of traditional procedures, hence interference with ancient vested rights. Reforms of the necessary sort were not very likely to come to the mind of a nobleman or a court favorite, and they would have seemed scandalous even to the boisterous young duke. Although von Kalb could not be expected to tamper seriously with aristocratic privileges, he did impose a head tax to which the nobility was subject. As for Goethe, he had very recently published ridicule of intellectuals who wished to impose newfangled schemes on a people and its customs, going so far as to call the aristocracy the only safeguard against such "despotism." Despite their good intentions, we shall not expect to credit the three young men who began to administer Saxe-Weimar in

1776 with any significant accomplishments. Our main interest lies in how an important share of responsibility for affairs of state affected Goethe's intellectual development. We can begin with a quick survey of Weimar's main problem areas.

The same diminutive size of the duchy which favored honest administration contributed to its chronic poverty. There was no manfacturing to speak of, nor could any have been profitably developed so long as export markets were choked by the doctrinaire mercantilism of the large states, England, France, Austria, and Prussia. The main industry was agriculture. Although there existed great demand for its products abroad, Weimar was remote and the roads in Germany unbelievably bad. In von Kalb's only export experiment, the price obtained for Weimar grain at the port of embarkation approximated the cost of transporting it there. To be sure, the grain was of exceptionally low quality, having been collected by Weimar in lieu of taxes.

Efforts to improve medieval cultivation methods were vigorously opposed by the nobility. It was generally agreed, for example, that the so-called three-field system, a primitive crop-rotation plan whereby centuries of cultivation and grazing had exhausted the soil, should be replaced by a method which would include soil-building crops like clover. But since the nobility possessed annual grazing rights on that third of the land which would presumably go to soil-building, no change could be effected.

Taxes were very modest by modern standards, but the taxing system was cumbersome in the extreme. According to that custom still widespread in the eighteenth century, yet so incomprehensible to our minds, collection was farmed out on a commission basis. Hence taxes were paid by some willingly, by others because the collector held a grudge against them, by still others not at all. Ultimate taxing authority lay with the Estates, whose sessions were dominated by the nobility. The only significant tax was the land tax, and the nobility, who held most of the land, were exempt from it.

Although small, Saxe-Weimar was itself a conglomerate of three older principalities, and any new tax had to be levied formally by the Estates in each. It is no wonder that von Kalb's courageous attempt to introduce an excise — this was a kind of tax favored by enlightened theory as both fair and humane — was at last unsuccessful, gaining him only considerable ill will. His unpopularity was eventually exceeded only by his ineptness in accountancy, and when Weimar was unable to pay interest on her debts in 1782, he was removed from office.

During the difficult months preceding von Kalb's removal Goethe became more and more deeply involved in Weimar's finances and was the natural choice to replace von Kalb. His handling of the 1782 crisis impresses us as revealing an easy grasp of Weimar's complicated affairs as well as considerable psychological astuteness in placating the Estates, who held the purse strings. An increased contribution to the bankrupt Chamber, he felt, could be avoided, thus making a new tax levy unnecessary. To be sure, the Estates' extraordinary subsidies of previous years would have to be continued for the time being. It was obvious that the Chamber had to be bailed out of its present embarrassment, but this could be accomplished if the Estates themselves would assume once and for all the total Weimar indebtedness of some 200,000 talers. As this debt was gradually amortized, the reduction in interest payments would accrue to the Estates, not to the Chamber, and a gradual reduction in taxes would result. As for how the Estates should meet the immediate added obligation, Goethe had an answer for that, too. He had served for three years now as head of the so-called War Commission, which was financed not by the Chamber, but by the Estates directly. In his capacity as commissioner of war he proposed radical reductions totaling nearly 30,000 talers annually. In this way the

Estates were given the hope of abolishing that irritating head tax instituted during the von Kalb regime, to which even the nobility had been subject.

A few of the figures involved in Goethe's stripping of the Weimar militia are revealing. Its Hussars (1 officer and 48 mounted police) were all retained as essential to the safety of the roads and rural districts. However, the artillery (1 officer and 8 men) was abolished and the infantry cut back sharply from 19 officers and 500 men to 6 officers and 136 men. In this way Goethe could claim to be cutting expenses in half (from 59,000 to 30,000 talers) so long as one did not figure in the pensions, which had to be increased initially (by 8,000 talers). He assured the Estates that this item would decline as time passed, but in order to make good the promise he had to curtail new enlistments. Within a few years the crime rate in Weimar reflected its inadequate police force; defense against foreign powers was, of course, out of the question. Ten years later, when the district of Eisenach had to lend its ten best men to help quell student disorders in Jena, only twenty-three men remained, all over fifty years old, and some of them in their seventies. Tiny principalities like Weimar — there were scores of them in the Holy Roman Empire — were not really viable political bodies any more, for they were capable neither of protecting themselves from enemies without nor of freeing themselves from ancient inherited injustices within.

We shall do well to guard against hasty judgment of Goethe as statesman, remembering that our thinking has been firmly prejudiced by the actual course of events in Europe in later years. From our point of view radical reform seems to have been the sole and obvious alternative to revolution. Goethe became more and more frustrated with the archaic system; as the years passed, he even sensed that violence was imminent in Europe, but he was not prepared even then to advocate radical change. He had no illusions about the ruling circles, and this meant that he knew the aristocracy too well to believe them capable of accepting even mild reforms. Hence he directed all his energies toward an efficient administration of the old machinery, apparently convinced, most of the time, that good government is not much different from good administration.

Eighteenth-century bureaucracy was notorious for its indirectness, periwigged parlor officials managing affairs through subalterns who themselves tried to keep their gloves clean. Policy was often formulated on the basis of inaccurate information, and the results were relayed back through unreliable channels. Carl August felt that this had been the case in Weimar during his mother's regency. Now, over the heads of her old experienced ministers, he ventured out into his territory to assess situations personally. Goethe is often credited with encouraging the boy in this, but a penchant for firsthand knowledge seems to have been one of Carl August's characteristics anyhow. It was more significant that he recognized in Goethe a sympathetic comrade whose powers of observation and judgment could be trusted. Here was one member of the Privy Council, at least, whose reports were sure to be factual and personally checked out. It became apparent that with his support the new sovereign could seek firmer, more direct control of the regime. In the 1770's the Privy Council still wielded considerable authority. Carl August usually presided over its biweekly meetings, and Goethe never missed a session. Over the years, however, it was reduced to an efficient board for routine matters, so that in the 1790's both Goethe and the duke had become virtual strangers to its meetings. Carl August's approval had to be obtained for expenditures exceeding 50 talers. This is an example of how policy-making was passed from the government to the prince during Goethe's tenure.

The gradual assertion of this goal is evidence of Goethe's careful judgment, and not that of the boy, who never really learned the discipline of long-range planning. In line with their strategy

Goethe had to take over a large number of specific commissions, usually in the capacity of troubleshooter, and not on an officially permanent basis: the Commission of Mines in 1776, pending the appointment of a minister of mines (1780); the Commission of War in 1779, when an emergency grew out of Frederick's request to levy troops in Saxe-Weimar; the Commission of Roads in the same year; the Chamber in 1782; the Tax Commission for Ilmenau in 1784; secret negotiations in behalf of the Union of Princes in 1785; and so on. In order to appreciate Goethe's tremendous usefulness we have to bear in mind that he was also constantly at hand as an implicitly trusted personal adviser. A diary entry, for example, from the summer of 1779: "Carl August came at ten. We spoke about things which can't be put into words — he had begun yesterday — internal questions of government, externals . . . concerning the court, his wife, how to understand other people. I explained why he has so much trouble with this and that, why he should not entangle himself so much in details. He stated his point of view, and a long, interesting discussion developed." Any prince was fortunate to have a counselor like this. Our own interest, however, lies in how these years affected Goethe's thinking about political issues. He could scarcely avoid relating his practical experience in Weimar to the enthusiastic theorizing of his *Götz* epoch. Can we expect those earlier notions to be rejected now, or at least to be matured somewhat?

If we consider his ten years of service before Italy (1776-86) from the point of view of their impact on his thinking, we are inclined to divide them into three periods. Initially, there was a time of "boundless personal ambition," as one observer called it,[1] ebullient devotion to Carl August and a rather dreamy general interpretation of his own career. As time passed Goethe had to take a more modest view of his political prospects, recognizing that they would in all likelihood be confined within the narrow limits of Saxe-Weimar, but he felt a growing sense of belonging and of responsibility to this land and its people. Therefore the second period was one of devotion to hard work. Finally, the last few years before Italy were characterized by an increasing frustration in the discharge of his duties and, toward the end, by a maddening sense of doom as he recognized that the circumstances which impeded his own effectiveness in Weimar were really only a deceptively favorable sampling of a Europe-wide, quite rotten system. The crystallization of his thinking on political matters during these years was important for the development of his mature outlook and for his approach to other subjects.

During the first wild months in Weimar he urged a Strasbourg friend not to pay any attention to the gossip he might hear about him — this was about the time of the Klopstock letter — because he was "firmly resolved neither to listen to what is said about me nor to heed advice. The outcome is not important, either. *Hoi polloi* looks for results, says a Greek, and to them the fortunate appear wise."[2] That is the remark of an *Originalgenie*, sure that his steps are charmed. "Like a sleigh ride goes my life, passing fast and jingling, promenading back and forth. God knows what I am destined for, that I am put through such schools as these."[3] He was still preoccupied with a notion of some benevolent destiny that assured his glorious future. "What fate has in store for me, that it puts me through all these schools, ~~it surely intends to place me where the usual torments of mankind can no longer hurt me. At this point I still regard all as preparation.~~ I crossed that out because it was expressed obscurely and indefinitely."[4] In the first weeks in Weimar he decided on a coat of arms for himself, the "morning star," as he called it, harbinger of the light to come. His motto was "All for love," and the morning star is, of course, Venus.

In these months he conceived Weimar as only a first stage in a grand, as yet unrevealed design. J. Heinrich Merck, the close Frankfurt friend who had helped finance the publication of *Götz* and who contributed large sums to Goethe's support in the expensive Weimar environment, received regular progress reports. He was the first to learn of Herder's appointment, and to him went also the first intimation of Goethe's own new position — three months before Carl August actually arranged it: "I have tried the court, now I will try government, and on to higher things."[5] Goethe was probably not clear himself as to just what the "higher things" might be. In the same letter to Merck occurs the light remark, "It is also fun to get to know a countryside so well." Although it did not mean anything more to him yet, this countryside and its peasants were gradually to win his love. They turned out to be the true destiny which determined much of his life and cast a final form on his political thinking.

From his first summer in Weimar we have a note in which he speaks of his feelings on returning from a short excursion: "I was suddenly struck by how dear the countryside is to me, the land! Ettersburg [overlooking Weimar], the insignificant hills! and it flashed through my soul: if you had to forsake all this, too. . . ."[6] He continues into a highly subjective vision so characteristic of the sentimental age that we may remain skeptical about its sincerity. But there is no question about the genuineness of his attachment to his little cottage on the Ilm, where he lived all that first summer and continued to spend as much time as he could. He had a garden, kept bees, set out trees on his hillside, and felt a true homesickness when he had to be away very long. Eventually a similar fondness extended to the rest of the land, but Goethe himself might not have been able to name the precise time when it captured him. We, who have just the papers to go by, can only make the observation that from a certain time and place a document survives in which he admits it. Prussia seems to have offered the occasion for the letter in question.

Realization of serious political ambitions, however vaguely conceived, would have had to take Goethe out of his Weimar

"school" to some grander court with real political power. Of the
two most obvious possibilities, Vienna was unlikely because he
was not a Catholic. Furthermore, Frederick's Prussia seemed,
from a distance anyway, to represent the kind of forward-think-
ing, expansionist regime which a young man of presumably un-
limited abilities could find attractive. For all of Goethe's life this
state had been the object of great popular interest and speculation,
even a source of German national pride, and we can scarcely
overestimate the eagerness with which he at last approached Berlin. It was on an official visit with Carl August in the spring of
1778. "Wörlitz, Thursday. After dinner we go to Potsdam, and
thence to Berlin. . . . Soon I shall be in the splendor of the royal
city and in the noise of the world with its preparation for war
[Prussia was on the brink of hostilities with Austria over the issue
of the Bavarian succession]. . . . I appear to be coming nearer and
nearer to the essence of drama as I become more and more affected by the way the great play with mankind, and the gods play
with the great."[7]

The impact of the court itself, however, was sobering and dis-
appointing. Experience in remote, tiny Weimar with its relatively
humane, close relationship between regime and subjects seems to
have provided Goethe with no basis for imagining what Frederick's monstrous machine would be like. He was shocked at the
lack of love with which Frederick's officials discussed the great
man, whom it was obviously no pleasure to serve. Few could hope
to be more than a small cog or, at best, a doll mounted on a
music box: "From the movements of the dolls you can infer those
of the hidden wheels, and especially of the big old cylinder
stamped 𝓕𝓡 with its thousand pegs that produces one tune
after another."[8] The longer he stayed, the more distasteful he
found the prospects of the civil servant here.

> I can tell you this much, the bigger the world the more disgust-
> ing the comedy, and I swear that no dirty joke or obscenity

from the Harlequinades is so revolting as the behavior of the great, middle-sized, and small when they come together. I have prayed to the gods that they keep me brave and honest to the end, and rather hasten my end than let me creep down the final stretch like a louse. But the value of this adventure for me, on the other hand, and for all of us, cannot be expressed in words. — I pray to the gods and feel the courage within me to swear eternal hatred of them if they behave toward me as their image [presumably the king] behaves toward man.[9]

This on the eve of his departure from Berlin. After a brief rest in Potsdam he felt his "soul purified," but was eager to get home again.[10] He let the Lady Charlotte know of his arrival with a note: "I wish you a good morning. My valley is dearer and more comfortable to me than the wide world. Last night I thought what a pretty picture the gods must think I am, since they seem to want me in such a priceless frame. I believe and feel that you love me. You and the duke dwell above me like hook and ribbon upholding the frame and the painting."[11]

It was in the months and years immediately following the visit to Berlin that Goethe took on his difficult and time-consuming offices and commissions in the Weimar regime. Gossips ceased to spread tales about excesses of boisterousness, but told one another instead about Goethe's lean appearance and wondered whether his health could hold up under the strain of so many duties. He calmed his mother's worries about such talk: "As to my situation, despite great difficulties there is much in it which is desirable for me, the best proof being that I cannot at present imagine any other for which I would exchange it . . . Merck and others judge my condition quite falsely in that they see only my sacrifices and not my profits. They cannot comprehend that I grow richer daily, in the act of devoting so much."[12] Obviously a great sobering had occurred during the Weimar service. We are able to date it in no better way than the paradoxical one of calling attention to

Goethe's first open admission of *ambition,* in his diary on May 13, 1780. "I am determined to become master of the situation. Only he who denies himself utterly is worthy of rule, or can rule." The point is that his ambition is now of a selfless kind which he is not at all ashamed of. His diary and his notes to Carl August from early 1781, for example, record how carefully he manipulated the War Commission until he was in full control of its affairs and able at last to conclude: "Now I would not be afraid to set a far greater department in order — even several — may God give me the opportunity and the courage." Since in each of his successive undertakings Weimar's confused finances constituted a major hindrance, he welcomed the opportunity to take full charge when von Kalb's resignation from the Chamber brought it to him. On this occasion we learn of a new motto adopted in recent years, for he has it placed above his door: *Hic est aut nusquam quod quaerimus* — "Here, or nowhere, is what we seek."[13]

We cannot expect Goethe to have expressed himself very fully in writing about how his sentimental devotion to Carl August waned during the same years when his more earthy affection for Weimar was growing. There is no significant negative remark until 1781, but by then his frustrations break forth in the two quite harsh statements already quoted: "His bold enterprises are only hare-brained larks ... he lacks judgment and true resolve" — "I am no longer in the least surprised that most hereditary rulers are so crazy, stupid and silly ... although the frog can exist on dry land for a time, he is made for the water."[14] These remarks make us suspect that Goethe had already been chafing for some time under Carl August's irresponsibility. Now his concern about the Chamber brought him into direct conflict with the duke and with aristocratic perquisites and prerogatives in general. "We are condemned to eat up the marrow of the land," he lamented, "blasting any benefit of plenty."[15]

One of his major cares was for agricultural methods. He brought in an English irrigation expert whose success especially delighted him: "I ride around with Batty, who has no theory, but whose accomplishments always correspond with my theory, and you may be assured that I take great pleasure from it. Then I survey all the hierarchy upwards and look back on the peasant, drawing the essentials from the earth. He would get along comfortably enough if he sweated for himself alone, but you know how, when the aphids have sucked themselves sleek and green on their rose branches, the ants come and draw the filtered juice out of their bellies. Thus it goes up the ladder to us, who have managed now to consume more in a day than can be produced below."[16] His troubles were to become greater, and remarks like this one grimmer, as when Voltaire's attack on Frederick caused him to wonder, in one of his few explicit references to "kings and princes," just when the world was going to open its eyes about them.[17] Certain comments might even be taken as a little ominous: "Our affairs are going tolerably well, but unfortunately nothing produces nothing. I know, all right, what ought to be done instead of all the busy work and proposals and resolutions."[18] But his typical tone is one of quiet resignation: "The common folk have to carry the sack, and it is pretty unimportant whether it weighs too much on the right shoulder or on the left."[19] Is it any wonder that he was exasperated when Carl August became interested in joining other petty princes in financing a military arm from Weimar's meager resources? We have a little farce from 1784 in which he lets a doctor tout the efficacy of a laxative:

> The power of the drink is famous far and wide,
> And its effect called *princely:*
> It forces its way through, leaves not a thing inside.[20]

Merck had observed that the whole secret as to why Goethe stayed in Weimar and why he was indispensable there lay in his love for the people with whom he lived.[21] Merck may have been referring to the circles of Carl August and the nobility, and not to Weimar's populace in general, but Goethe often expressed his fondness for the common folk with eloquence. He once wrote from a village near Weimar: "The whole way I have felt like a man who leaves a city where he long drank out of a fountain on the square, into which all the springs of the region flow. Then at last one day on a walk he comes to one of these springs at its source, and he cannot get his fill of watching this eternally bubbling thing, and he takes pleasure in the weeds and rocks."[22] As he became better acquainted with the Weimar populace, his earlier organic perception of countryside and people was not changed, but verified and expanded. When a friend followed his suggestion to take up mineralogical studies, Goethe congratulated him in a most startling but typical way: "You are on the right path and you will also see how necessary those first fundamental concepts are on which I rely, and which I recommend for easy and accurate judgment of important new natural and cultural phenomena. Man is so closely related to his habitat that considering the latter is sure to enlighten us about the inhabitant."[23]

In terminology of a later day, Goethe would be called a political conservative for two theoretical reasons. He continued to believe in national and regional character as qualities which ought to be nurtured by government, and he regarded the local aristocracy — despite the disadvantages, with which he was only too familiar — as best suited to developing and protecting native institutions. The term "conservative" may seem most appropriate, however, on account of his extreme practical skepticism about political reform: "By God there is not a scribe in Chancellery who cannot talk more sense in a quarter hour than I can carry out in a quarter year, God knows in ten years."[24] He took this same position repeatedly — here is a cooler expression of it: "In civic matters, where everything proceeds in a definite order, it is possible neither to hasten the good significantly, nor to dislodge this or that evil. They have to go together into the fold like black and white sheep of the same flock."[25]

As *Götz* had given artistic form to his immature political views, Goethe's more considered position would eventually go into the drama *Egmont*. It was begun during *Götz* and *Werther* days, but only about two acts seem to have been completed then. He took it up again in the years around 1780 and made enough progress that he could send a copy to Justus Möser for his opinion.[26] It is unfortunate that none of these early versions has survived, because they would be very interesting for the information they might offer, not so much about the drama itself as about these fertile periods in Goethe's life: the early 1770's and the years just before and after 1780, when all of his important works were either conceived or revised. The *Egmont* manuscript which he took with him to Italy may have been in a fairly well finished form, since he did not expect it to make any very great demands: "My revised *Iphigenia* is going off today. Now I will finish up *Egmont* so that it at least appears to be complete."[27] But he was wrong. The work on *Egmont* turned out to be of an entirely different order, in that it called for some new writing, not merely revising and recasting as had been the case with *Werther* and *Iphigenia*. Furthermore, this subject was one on which his opinions had been affected by experience over the years, so that it was not at all easy to make the new match the old.

Here in Italy he also felt a detachment from political theories and problems. For the time being he set *Egmont* aside and turned to another drama, *Tasso*. It was of a more subjective nature, like *Iphigenia,* a perception which he believed to be essentially integrated and wanting only polished form. As it turned out, *Tasso* was also years from completion, but this was the manuscript which he carried along with him on his visit to Naples at the end of February and onward by sea to Sicily in April. On the voyage he suffered from fever and delirium, caused in all likelihood by malaria from the then notorious swamps north of Naples.[28] He crossed Sicily from Palermo to Agrigento, then crossed the island again eastward to Catania and went up the coast to Messina, whence he shipped back to Naples in the middle of May.

In all, he spent about six weeks in Sicily. It seems to have left with him the immediate impression of tremendous fertility combined with natural hostility — both Catania and Messina had just suffered those terrible earthquakes which resulted in the building of entirely new cities. He did not fail to notice a certain grotesqueness in landscape and art, matched by pomp and arbitrariness in government (Palermo had a very eccentric prince and Messina a madcap English governor). All was set against the great depths of time which the magnificent temples in Agrigento opened up before him, and viewed with a sometimes sickly and feverish eye quite uncharacteristic of Goethe. In the *Italian Journey* he places the generally dismal impression in a humorous light by connecting it with what he took to be his own queasy sea legs when he left Messina: "I was victim again to the unpleasant sensation of seasickness, and now the condition was not mitigated, as it had been on the trip over, by the comfort of seclusion. . . . Actually, we had seen nothing but utterly vain exertions of humankind to maintain themselves against the violence of nature, the insolent treachery of time, and the curse of their own divisiveness. Carthaginians, Greeks, Romans and so many successors have built and destroyed. Selinunt was ruined methodically; to lay low the temples of Agrigento, two millennia did not suffice; for Catania and Messina, a few hours or moments were enough. I refused to yield to these truly seasick reflections of a man being rocked to and fro on the wave of life."[29] Yet the impression was strong, reawakening older political reflections now on an entirely new level from which the vanity of all man's institutions seemed apparent. Back in Naples he wrote: "The more I see of the world, the less I am able to hope that humanity can ever become a wise, intelligent, happy mass. Perhaps among the million worlds there is one which can claim such excellence; the constitution of this one is such that I entertain as little hope for it as I do for Sicily."[30] His point of view is clearly one which places no great faith in any particular interpretation of governmental responsibility or purpose.

In June he returned to Rome and to the problem of finding a cool spot for the hot months. July and August were spent at work on *Egmont*. It was to take on a more artistically polished form, but Goethe also allowed himself new hopes with respect to its contents. He saw the possibility of presenting fundamental political questions from a vantage point detached enough to interest men "who lead and have led important and involved careers."[31]

The dashing Egmont, tragic hero of the Dutch in their sixteenth-century struggle against Spanish domination, is still very obviously Goethe's youthful perception of a brilliant national leader. Egmont makes it even clearer than Götz had that he acts spontaneously in accordance with his character, and the Dutch are confident that he is fully in tune with their own nation. The antagonist, the Spanish Duke of Alba, is a foreign despot with no understanding for local traditions, and at the same time a cool rationalist who intends to change their ways.

The famous fourth act is the only part which we know Goethe to have written in Rome. Almost all of it goes to a fine debate in which Egmont argues his view of the people as an organic entity which should develop along the lines of its native traditions, while Alba represents the rational meliorism popular among eighteenth-century theoreticians. But the treacherous Spaniard allows the discourse to take place only because his men are in the meanwhile securing the palace and making Egmont his prisoner.

The drama closes on the eve of Egmont's execution. While he lies sleeping, his vision of Freedom appears on the stage. It is not freedom in any modern political sense of the word. As in *Götz,* political freedom to Goethe apparently still meant freedom to remain in character, guided by the benevolent paternalism of a local aristocracy who speak the same dialect as the peasant — freedom therefore *from* the imposition of foreign ideas, including intellectual schemes for more efficient government.

Goethe had after all dreamed fondly of improvements in Weimar and worked ten years for them. His experience is obvious in Egmont's projection of how a new regent in the Netherlands might conduct affairs: "He'd come with great plans, projects, and ideas as to how he will straighten everything out, arrange and maintain it. Today he'd be busy with this trifle, tomorrow with another one, the next day encounter that obstacle, spend one month perfecting his plans, another in bitterness about his failures, half a year with disorder in a single province. Time will get away from him, too; his head will spin while affairs go on in their old course — and he, instead of crossing the wide seas in accordance with a line drawn on a chart, will thank God if he can keep his ship off the rocks in the present storm."

Although the good-humored resignation of these lines may bespeak day-to-day administrative experience in Weimar, the point of view is not really different from that of the younger, inexperienced Goethe. It is generally true of his political thinking that fundamental premises were not rejected during the Weimar years. His tolerance of the aristocracy and the feudal system survived bitter disappointments with them.

All this seems important because Goethe's politics constitute our very earliest example of serious speculative thinking on his part. The young genius had apprehended the Strasbourg Cathedral in doctrinaire anti-rationalism: "My soul swelled with one entire, great impression which, consisting of a thousand harmonious particulars, could be tasted and enjoyed, but by no means understood or explained." With exactly the same *intuitive* process, he thought he could reduce a thousand particularities of tradition and region to the harmonious perception of Alsatian, then of German, national character. We have seen that his mature assessment of the Italians was not essentially different from this. The young Goethe actually argued that, in order to perceive the "entirety," his own mental state needed to be kept *dumpf,* or "dreamy" — i.e., with access to subconscious, nonrational modes of apprehension — and the older man would not have disagreed. Although his political views had been refined and clarified in Weimar, they had also become hardened there; and although he gained distance and detachment while in Italy and Sicily, his old idea of national character remained, if we can judge by *Egmont,* essentially the same as in Strasbourg. Political thinking which is based on the preservation and organic development of national character tends to be conservative.

NOTES

1. Count Putbus to Count Wartensleben, July, 1776. Bode, 206.
2. To Zimmermann on March 6, 1776.
3. To Johanna Fahlmer on November 22, 1775.
4. To Auguste von Stolberg on May 18, 1776.
5. March 8, 1776.
6. To Charlotte on July 16, 1776.
7. To Charlotte on May 14, 1778.
8. To Charlotte on May 17, 1778.
9. To Charlotte on May 19, 1778.
10. To Charlotte on May 21, 1778.
11. To Charlotte on June 2, 1778.
12. August 11, 1781.
13. To Merck on July 16, to Knebel on July 27, 1782.
14. For full quotations and sources, see pp. 5 and 6.
15. To Charlotte on April 3, 1782.
16. To Knebel on April 17, 1782.
17. To Charlotte on June 5, 1784.
18. To Charlotte on June 9, 1784.
19. To Herders on June 20, 1784.
20. *Scherz List und Rache. JA* 8, 110.
21. To Wieland on August 8, 1778. Bode, 241.
22. To Charlotte on March 5, 1779.

23. To Knebel on December 30, 1785.
24. Diary, May 13, 1780.
25. To Charlotte on September 21, 1780.
26. To Jenny von Voigts on May 5, 1782.
27. To Carl August on January 13, 1787.
28. Werners *Tagebuch* for May 7, 1810. Herwig, 421.
29. *Italienische Reise,* May 14, 1787.
30. Ibid., May 17, 1787.
31. To Carl August on November 17, 1787.

Nature Studies

Goethe's broad range of inquiry into natural forms eventually became much subtler and more self-critical than his political speculations, perhaps because the later efforts profited from those earliest attempts at independent judgment. Nevertheless, we find a strikingly similar pattern throughout, and we are inclined to think that his satisfaction with an intuitive approach to political theory may have been the determining factor. Into old age Goethe believed that the perception of total *Gestalt* was decisive in most areas of inquiry. From those early speculations into national character and art, through his studies in anatomy, geology, botany, and, in the post-Italian years, optics, we find that metaphor still applicable in which patient accumulation of "wood and straw" is at last rewarded by a flash of general comprehension for a whole context, "one entire, great impression." For him the intuitive insight remained the whole point of his study. The subsequent development of most of the natural sciences has for this reason led to fundamental differences between his conception of nature study and our own.

Modern science conceives itself as a method for developing models to comprehend natural phenomena in quantitative terms. The successive models may indeed possess aesthetic value in themselves, but they are expected to be of immediate practical use or to contribute to further investigation. As more accurate or more comprehensive models are developed, older ones become obsolete — in the scientific view, worthless. For Goethe science was not a method at all, but a process, like art. Science and art seemed to him to be quite normal and necessary behavioral patterns by which man tries to come to terms with the outer world. Each individual attempt has to be judged in terms of its content and inner integrity more than for its results, which have no universal validity.

His first intense occupation with natural forms was in sketching and painting. He was exceptionally clever in capturing a likeness, be it in portraiture or landscape. According to an anecdote from the early Weimar days he once stepped outside with pad and pencil, sketched in a few quick lines representing the back of the head and shoulders of a sitting figure, displayed his drawing to his friends inside, and asked what they thought this figure was doing. When all declared without hesitation that he was eating, Goethe proudly led them out and showed them his model, sitting there with his back turned, eating.[1] He had obviously discovered some characteristic posture in people eating. The anecdote accurately reflects what most delighted Goethe both in science and in art.

As a youth in Strasbourg he had elevated ideas about characteristic features to the level of theory. It was a basically artistic conviction that inner nature has to express itself in external form. He contributed sketches and essays to Johann Caspar Lavater's popular work on physiognomy, which remained a standard work for judging human character well into the nineteenth century. In Goethe's last years at home in Frankfurt he consciously or unconsciously extended his notions about characteristic features from the realm of art criticism to nature in general. Eventually they came to condition his thinking to such an extent that the aged Goethe urges us to seek nothing at all "behind the phenomena. They are themselves the theory."[2] Perhaps most revealing of his conception of science in this regard is a remark which he made in discussing his botanical studies: "In every epoch scientific men have felt the drive to recognize living forms as such, to apprehend their external, visible, tangible parts in context, to perceive them as indicators of what is within, and in this way to form a conception of the whole. I do not need to argue how closely related this scientific desire is to the artistic and imitative drive."[3]

The human form was of special interest to Goethe as artist, but eighteenth-century Germany held few opportunities for observing the undraped figure; hence he welcomed the chance to study anatomy at the nearby University of Jena in 1780. During the winter of 1781-82, he himself conducted biweekly lectures on anatomy for artists at the Weimar Art Academy. The decision to do so marks the beginning of a most important stage in the development of his thinking. Here for the first time in his life he was compelled to master a subject thoroughly and in detail. He called his anatomy professor, Justus Christian Loder, "the most energetic and helpful person in the world. . . . This week he helped me cover osteology and myology. Two unfortunates, luckily for us, died, and we have pretty much peeled them down and helped them out of their sinful flesh."[4] Such opportunities as this one or, as on another occasion with Loder, the dissection of a human fetus were by no means commonplace in the eighteenth century. Goethe's work with Loder became fairly basic, extended into physiology (e.g., experiments with gastric acid), and continued for four or five years. Never before had he pursued any study with such persistence, energy, and expense. By the fall of 1782 he had begun to focus on comparative osteology, the branch which would henceforth retain his main interest. Before the year was out he had begun what was to be an extensive collection of animal skeletons and would include exotic specimens like the elephant, rhinoceros, and walrus. By 1783 at the very latest he was exploring their relationships among one another and to their prehistoric cousins.

This meant that Goethe had become one of those who did not accept the still popular prefiguration theory, which derived all species on earth from similar forebears as created by the Lord and reported in Genesis. It was extremely important for the future course of his scientific work that his very first systematic independent research brought him immediately into conflict with a generally accepted theory which seemed to him to have no bearing at all on experience. He had already shown marked distrust of the intellectuals of his day, but this had been on political and cultural issues, in the last analysis imponderables. Now, in an empirical field, learned opinion again struck him as absurd. His further experience in comparative anatomy, and later in his botanical studies, finally convinced him that "professional scholars," as he contemptuously called them, must be out of all touch with reality. "They are not interested in the living concept, but only in what has been said about it."[5]

This distrust had its effect on his own thought processes. He came to regard deduction as questionable, most general explanations as deceptive, and the experts as too prejudiced by their hard-won theoretical positions to be capable of impartial consideration of new contributions. Schiller, who visited the Weimar circle during the summer while he was away in Italy, reported that Goethe's spirit had stamped them all: "A proud philosophical contempt of all speculation and investigation, a fondness for nature which is carried so far as to be affected, and an appeal to the five senses — in short, a certain childish simplicity of mind characterizes the entire local sect. They would rather collect herbs or minerals than become entangled in a line of reasoning."[6] Goethe admits as much with his advice from Rome to his faithful representative in Weimar, Philipp Seidel: "You do very well, my dear man, to occupy yourself with the study of nature. Just as the most natural pleasures are the best, the most natural studies are the best, too. Your observations are very good; you are proceeding in a way which favors observation. You must just take care not to place too much value in your inferences. I do not want to say that you should make no inferences, because that is the nature of the mind. You must just always think less highly of your opinion than of your eye."[7]

The scientific theory which had done more than anything else to set Goethe's mind in this manner was that of prefiguration and separate creation of species, according to which man's skull structure, for example, was viewed as so fundamentally different from that of other mammals that he had to be regarded as an independent species since the time of Adam. Whereas the upper jaw in most mammals extends to form some kind of snout and is complex, in man it appears as a solid bone. Herder, at work on his *Ideas for a Philosophy of the History of Man,* in which he speculated about a common origin for all life, received from Goethe the following excited note in March, 1784: "I have found — neither gold nor silver, but something that gives me unspeakable pleasure — the intermaxillary bone in man! Loder and I were comparing human and animal skulls; I came upon its traces and, lo, it is there. Only, I beg you not to tell anyone, because it has to be worked out in secret. You too will take great pleasure in it, because it is like a keystone to man. It's not missing, it is there, too! And how!"[8]

Goethe had succeeded in tracing out the sutures which betray the fusion of man's upper jaw out of components identifiable with those found in other mammals, and he was working toward a theory of homology of parts. The big job which had to be "worked out in secret" could now begin: collection of a sufficiently wide variety of skulls, drawing them and preparing copper engravings in a manner clear and convincing enough to persuade the scientific community of data which would compel them to rethink their conception of species. Goethe was by no means alone in his convictions. The accepted account of the history of the earth and of life on it was being challenged in these years on many fronts. A Frenchman, F. Vicq d'Azyr, had published Goethe's same observation about the upper jaw a year earlier. Goethe did not know about him, and certainly Goethe's was the more extensive and resolute attempt to convince his contemporaries. However, fundamental reorientations in scientific thinking are essentially generation problems. The old generation of scientists does not change its mind; they just die out while a younger generation goes its new way. None of those who received the carefully illustrated copies of Goethe's paper accepted his finding.

Goethe had actually anticipated this situation and had tried to avoid it by separating the existence of the premaxilla in man from the implications of its presence. He explained this to a friend in sending him a copy: "I have refrained from letting the result become apparent . . . namely, that there is no specific difference to be found between man and animal but that man is on the contrary most closely related to the animals. The correlation of all parts makes each creature what it is, and man is man just as much by virtue of the form and nature of his upper jaw as by virtue of the form and nature of the last segment of his little toe he is man. Similarly, each creature is in turn only a variant of a great harmony which has to be investigated in its entire extent, otherwise each individual is a dead letter."[9] Implied in these remarks are thoughts which were to occupy Goethe for years to come.

From the point of view of "a great harmony," collection of specimens seemed tremendously important. The relationship not only of mammals but eventually of all life was to be revealed by arranging individual specimens in such a way as to display each as an infinitely small variation on its nearest neighbors. Goethe was not beyond suggesting that life itself could be placed in a similar relationship to the rest of nature, which he was loath to call *an*organic. If our way of thinking seems to converge with his on this point, we must be all the more cautious about noting the fundamental differences. Our understanding of the relationships among life forms is historically oriented, and we inevitably visualize them in some kind of family tree. Surviving species take on major importance. They not only determine the shape of the tree; their forebears are construed in terms of modern forms, even though they may in fact have produced a larger number of lines which do not lead down to the present. Interpreting a structure in terms not drawn from the structure itself, said Goethe, is always a little like assuming that the dear Lord created the cork tree so that we can stop our bottles.

It was in the historical sense that Darwin's explanation for the survival of certain forms was accepted as a theory of evolution. Goethe's orientation is that of a mind still grappling with the great variety of forms that confront it, and seeking some preliminary mode of coming to terms with them. He is by no means yet prepared to investigate the survival of specific ones, but directs his concern almost solely toward how they might have originated.

His first step was the visualization of a preliminary model for relating various structures among one another. The pattern which emerged in his mind was not the linear one of parent-offspring relationship, but a kind of radial arrangement of individuals and species around ideal types, "a general image in which the forms of all animals would be potentially subsumed and according to which each animal could be described in an appropriate manner. This type would have to be set up as far as possible in physiological terms. The general idea of a type precludes from the outset using any individual animal as a model."[10] Here we are quoting, to be sure, from the draft of a 1795 essay which may reflect his experience in fields yet to be discussed. Nevertheless, it is characteristic of his thinking as we have come to know it already, insofar as his *type* could be arrived at only by intuitive processes. He refused, for example, to accept developmental criteria:

> We therefore visualize the animal as a little self-contained world which exists by and for itself. Thus each creature constitutes its own purpose, and since all its parts have a specific reciprocal relationship among one another whereby the life process is maintained, each animal has to be regarded as physiologically perfect. From the point of view of internal economy none of its parts is useless. . . . Although it is true that certain parts may appear useless from an external point of view, because the inner conformation of the animal's nature shaped them in a certain way without reference to externals. Hence in the future we shall not ask, as for example with respect to the tusks of the walrus: what purpose do they serve? We shall ask: where do they come from? We shall not assert that horns are given the bull so that he can gore, but we shall investigate how he can have horns to gore with.[11]

This kind of question, accurately recognized by Goethe as belonging to the future, seemed to him to pertain to the inner economy of the organism. He felt that the most important guidelines for its investigation were the homology of parts and a law of compensation which sets limits to the development of individual organs. He was greatly impressed by the adaptability of the organism — for example:

> The bony structures are part of the organic whole. They cannot be considered in isolation, but are connected with all the other semi-hard and soft parts. These other parts are more or less related to the skeleton and are subject to ossification. We see this clearly in the development of the bones before and after the birth of the growing animal, where the membranes, cartilage, and bone masses take form gradually; we see it in elderly people and in pathological conditions where certain parts not by nature

included in the skeleton ossify and become a part of it, as it were, extending it. Nature has reserved precisely this process in the development of species in order to put bone masses here and there where some have only muscles and tendons.[12]

While he was acutely aware of the close interrelationship between species and natural environment, Goethe never appears to have thought in terms of natural selection. Since his concern was for how adaptations originate, he was struggling with questions which have only in recent decades come to the fore in genetics. He was especially impatient with those who tried to explain adaptations in terms of purposefulness or usefulness, because he felt that this was missing the point and prejudicing the investigation. Those who came after Darwin, for example, were content to note that some herbivorous animals develop horns for defense or for use in mating season. Goethe considered it more profitable to observe that horned animals do not produce tusks or fangs, because he hoped that an insight of this sort pertained to the inner economy of the organism.

Goethe's interest in geology went back to his very earliest Weimar days. However, it amounted to "dragging up wood and straw" which was not ignited until a fresh wind from his anatomical studies blew in the early 1780's. At that time his geology began to acquire a certain scientific character, although we must remember that this science was itself still in its infancy.

The very first of his special assignments in Weimar was that of the Commission of Mines at Ilmenau in the Thuringian forest south of Weimar. The old silver mines there had been closed for generations and, as in numerous similar areas in Europe, the population had emigrated or turned to glass-blowing, toy-making, etc. It was one of the most economically depressed sections of the duchy. Goethe and von Kalb formed the rather hare-brained scheme of reopening the old shafts. Many years later, in *Faust II,* the elderly poet gently satirized a similar situation: a self-seeking adviser to a somewhat fatuous sovereign holds out the promise of buried treasure as an overnight solution to chronic financial difficulties. The ores from Ilmenau proved barely rich enough to attract a few stockholders and lure them into throwing good money after bad. Not until better safety equipment became available in the nineteenth century did it become possible to work at depths which had long since been given up as unprofitable and dangerous. Goethe rued his project soon enough, but not before various hereditary interests, stockholders, outside experts, and miners with their families had become involved. Like the magician's apprentice, he had started something which could not so easily be curtailed, even by occasional tragedies. It was not until successive disasters in 1795 and 1796 that the shafts were closed down and an episode ended which had been of no benefit to the Weimar economy, albeit a sound lesson to the youngest member of its Privy Council.

The Thuringian Mountains with their striking geological formations and confusing variety of minerals were tremendously stimulating for a fellow who had spent his youth in the Rhein-Main basin. The diary from his 1775 trip to Switzerland records only subjective impressions made by the grandeur of the Alps. From his trip there in 1779, however, he brought back a collection of rock samples. His expensive mining operations had in the interval given him a practical reason, even an obligation, to scrutinize natural formations as objectively as he could. At first it was just a matter of gaining enough competence to help save the mining venture, and his knowledge of geology remained superficial. But he did become aware of differences in rock formations, learn to associate certain kinds of rocks with certain regions, and study the stratification of the earth's crust in mountainsides, in mines, and in the deeper salt shafts just now being drilled in Central Europe. He was extremely fortunate to acquire as his chief of mining operations young Carl Wilhelm Voigt, who had studied in Freiberg with the father of modern geology, Abraham Werner. Voigt wrote to his teacher in 1780 that, while no one in Weimar had any understanding of mineralogy, Goethe had at least shown interest in his, Voigt's, rock collection.[13] By the fall of this year the two were preparing geological maps of the whole area south and west of Weimar as far away as Würzburg, Fulda, and Hessia, and Goethe was becoming acquainted with the most recent literature in the field. To his friend Merck he expressed the hope that soon "one single great man who can make his way around the world either with his feet or with his intellect will be able to form, once and for all, a concept of this strangely constructed sphere, and describe it."[14]

This same letter, which characterizes the earliest progress in geology, also mentions the discovery of old volcano craters in Thuringia. Here lay the weak point of the Werner school, which minimized the importance of vulcanism. Perhaps because of the influence of Voigt and Werner, Goethe never gained a proper conception of igneous rocks; this became the fundamental error which prevented his ever attaining a clear view of the earth's history. Since he was sure that natural phenomena could be accounted for in terms with which man was familiar, in general laws observable throughout nature, any adduction of extraordinary circumstances and unfamiliar conditions seemed suspect to him. Hence he could not accept the terrific temperature fluctuations implied by volcanic action. He recognized that prehistoric epochs in the earth's history differed from historical ones, but only gradually, he felt, and by processes still observable today. In later years he came to speak of his "principle of constancy."

By about the time of his Italian trip he began to admit to himself that his geological ideas included irreconcilable contradictions. He observed, for example: "I cannot come a single step ahead in mineralogy without chemistry. I have known that for a long time, and that is why I put it aside — but I continue to be pulled and torn in that direction."[15] From a scientific point of view geology is perhaps the least significant of Goethe's nature studies, but it occupies an important place in the context of his personal development. His approach to geology corresponds well with his essentially intuitive grasp of other complex groups of phenomena. When he sent a collection of samples and maps to the Duke of Gotha toward the end of 1780, he stated: "In this affair, as in a thousand similar ones, intuitive comprehension (*der anschauende Begriff*) is infinitely preferable to rational understanding (*der wissenschaftliche Begriff*). When I stand upon, before, or within a mountain, observe the shape, the quality, and magnitude of its strata and veins, and visualize the components and form in a natural condition of flux, with the vivid perception *this is the way it originated* — how little can I convey of that feeling with samples and cross-sections."[16] Furthermore, precisely because he was unable to penetrate beyond the surface phenomena, the geological studies reinforced Goethe's skepticism about abstract theories, thus influencing his later studies.

Our first evidence that he was developing a more or less comprehensive view of the history of the earth occurs in connection with his early speculations about comparative anatomy. He wrote to Merck in 1782:

I know how to recite my osteology by heart, bone by bone. On any animal skeleton I can immediately discover the parts and call them by the name which has been given to their counterpart in man.... All the remains of bones that you mention, which can be found everywhere in the upper strata of the earth, are, as I am fully convinced, from the most recent epoch, although it is tremendously ancient in our customary way of reckoning time. In this epoch the ocean had already receded, but the rivers were wider and flowed at a level nearer that of the ocean.... As the sea level dropped, these alluvial plains were gradually drained, and the rivers dug out small beds down the middles. In that era elephants and rhinoceri inhabited the European plateaus; their remains were often washed down by mountain currents into the broad river valleys or coastal plains. Here they were more or less imbued with rock juices and preserved, so as to come to light now under a plow or by some other accident. . . . Soon the day will come when fossils will no longer be mixed at random, but arranged in accordance with the ages of the earth.[17]

Goethe's thinking here reflects quite accurately the history of geology, whose early decades were strongly influenced by an increasing appreciation of the fossil evidence as it rapidly accumulated from canalization and other excavations attending industrialization of England and Western Europe. There had been a tendency to account for the many extinct species thus attested by assuming that they had been victims of Noah's flood. It is indeed humbling to observe how an independent, even rebellious spirit like Goethe's is still inclined to explain so much in terms of high water. As we shall see, he continued to visualize the entire history of the earth, past and future, in terms of a continuous settling and recession of the primeval ocean — although he did not at all accept the traditional "flood" theory of fossils. We are amused, for example, when he remarks in Venice that the long-range problem of this city will be to keep its canals and harbor dredged as the sea level drops away. The visitor to Venice in our time sees the magnificent buildings seriously menaced in exactly the opposite way.

Goethe's decisive breakthrough in comparative anatomy occurred in March, 1784, this being the period when he was most intensely occupied with the collection of samples to fortify his contention about the upper jaw. In June he went to Eisenach to accept delivery on an elephant skull from the University of Göttingen, reporting to Herder that he was delighted with how well it confirmed his ideas. He goes on: "I have been busily climbing around on the rocks and have found a lot that I can use. I also believe that I have discovered a quite simple principle, or rather that I have applied the principle in such a way that it fully explains the formation of the larger masses."[18] In the fall, when the treatise on the intermaxillary bone was out of the way, he and Fritz von Stein made a field trip into the Harz Mountains for the purpose of collection and observation, apparently convinced that he was on the heels of a comprehensive geological theory. When he returned, he tutored his young companion in "the two first formative epochs of the earth, according to my new system."[19]

The second of Goethe's epochs is probably that of the broad rivers and high sea level described above in the letter to Merck. The first epoch, if we can judge from some of his notes in 1785, was that in which a primeval sea still held all substances in solution. We probably need to visualize some origin of the solar system like that propounded by Kant and later by La Place, a slow gravitation and concentration of matter originally widely dispersed: "When our earth formed as a body, its mass was in a more or less fluid state. This mass was not simple, but its components were in solution with one another. The solution had occurred by an inner heat, or rather the mass was maintained in a uniform solution by inner heat which far exceeded the temperature of melted metals. The core of the earth crystallized, and probably possesses the heaviest mass. The external crust of the core is granite." Crystallization and sedimentation do not appear to be entirely distinct processes in Goethe's mind.

> Thus from this general solution granite was the first precipitate, the first crystallization. This by no means yet cleared the tremendous ocean or purified it. All the parts which go to make up granite, together with an equal number of volatile parts, still darkened the water. The most volatile ones floated above the waters in the atmosphere, and there was a reciprocal exchange.

The first epoch of granite is simple and general over the entire earth. What precipitated after granite was a tremendous mass of lime and mica, which covers the granite everywhere to a certain depth. This was also very widespread, but not so uniform. This precipitation occurred in the water immediately after the granite had crystallized, because we find this kind of rock intermingled with granite, indeed alternating with it. Gneiss is the granite which precipitated out of the water after the first primary formation (*Grundbildung*), hence its striated form.[20]

The "quite simple principle" which Goethe thought he had applied successfully to the history of the earth included this notion of precipitation of rock masses out a primeval sea, but the principle itself was probably a yet broader perception which transcended his geological studies. In the same letter which reports tutoring Fritz on the earth's epochs, he resolves to keep on "meditating and investigating my friends the mountains so as to strengthen my faith." His rock collection became more and more extensive, on the same assumption which underlay his work with the upper jaw structure. He liked to speak of a *Suite* or a *Folge,* a succession of samples to be displayed in such a way as to reveal each as a variant on some central type. He had concluded that granite was the rock form to which all others must be related, for they all were originally formed from those same materials which had attained a *Grundbildung,* or kind of ideal balance, in granite. Formed in what he took to be the primary epoch of the earth's history and still reaching from its core to its highest peaks, granite constituted for him one of the givens with which the student of nature must come to terms, and beyond which he cannot penetrate. The attempt to go beyond such fundamentals leads off into a kind of abstraction which would not really further man's understanding of his own relationship to natural forms. Thus it was in the geological studies that Goethe probably first got the notion of an *Urphänomen,* a kind of archetype which stands, as it were, at the ideal center of all the other forms which nature has been able to derive from it. We shall see that this idea was to have great influence on his later studies, although his confidence in his success in geology waned with the passage of time.

"Natural things," he once observed to the Duke of Gotha, "all flow together, so that once you have embarked you are carried on by the current."[21] The approach which had by now become characteristic for Goethe was to prove most appropriate and productive in botany. Our first evidence of his increasing curiosity about plants is his watching beans sprout in the spring of 1785. He also made some investigations with the microscope about this time and spoke of "right nice discoveries and combinations which straighten out and clarify a lot of things, but I don't really know what to do with them."[22] The science was in those days still at the stage where nomenclature seemed the major problem, the development of proper categories for grouping like with like appearing to many to be the beginning and end of a therefore rather gloomy branch of natural history. Goethe recalled that even this aspect of botany had been made attractive to him by the quick mind of a congenial young man, Friedrich Gottlieb Dietrich. We are reminded of the importance of young Voigt for Goethe's early mineralogical work when we read his recollection of his meeting with Dietrich in June, 1785: "As a well-built youth with pleasant and regular features, he strode forward full of young strength and enjoyment in his mastery of the world of plants, his happy memory retaining all the strange designations and recovering them for his use at will. His presence appealed to me, his open and free character apparent from his bearing and actions, so that I was persuaded to take him with me on my trip to Carlsbad. On the way he seized eagerly and alertly on every herb, flower and blossom, bringing each specimen to the coach and naming it on the spot, and it opened up a new life for me in this delightful world."[23]

He always liked to think of botany as his comfort in troubled times. He undertook this first trip to Carlsbad because his health had become so poor; indeed, the journey there was interrupted by a kidney attack. On his way home he heard of the Necklace Affair. We know how the burden of official duties seemed heavy and hopeless in the fall. In these same months he had to accept the fact that the experts were not going to recognize his work on the intermaxillary bone, and he had to admit his own inadequate background for meaningful geological investigations. In September he took forth the *Genera Plantarum* by Carl von Linné; during the subsequent months he studied this first comprehensive taxonomy of plants. He later counted the Swedish scientist among the three writers (the other two being an Englishman, Shakespeare, and the Dutch Jew, Spinoza) who had exerted the greatest influence on him.[24] If this statement is correct, then he must have found in the *Genera Plantarum* a promise that beneath the stuffy nomenclature there lay a fresh aspect of nature with aesthetic charm and an intellectual challenge. Here he might yet hope to achieve the all-important overview, a "sure perception" of nature's plan.*

In the prolific records which he kept as he entered Italy, notes about plants and even sketches of leaf and seed forms are prominent. Already in Padua he was discovering "fine confirmation of my botanical ideas."[25] Although he was mainly occupied with art history, explicitly observing more than once that it had supplanted his scientific studies, the North European remained constantly aware of the varied new plant world through which he was passing. The long fall growing season struck him, and he was delighted to see new blossoms already in February. "Tell Herder that my botanical hypotheses are being definitely borne out and that I am on the way to the discovery of fine new relationships."[26]

We can only guess what these hypotheses might be, but since remarks of this sort are usually addressed to Herder, with whom he was accustomed to discuss the broad general principles of his studies, it seems likely that he is referring to his old quest for some ideal common denominator among natural forms. The archetypal plant, the *Urpflanze*, must have been a frequent subject of their conversations.

Immediately after the spring carnival of 1787, Goethe and Tischbein set off for the south, spending March in Naples. They climbed Vesuvius, visited Pompeii and Herculaneum. Goethe recalled being occupied with plants during this entire trip, but he probably had more time and attention for them after leaving Tischbein and sailing to Sicily. His *Italian Journey* brings the following record from Palermo in April: "In confrontation with so many new and renewed structures, my old whim came back to me, could I not discover the *Urpflanze* among this host? There must be such a thing. How else would I recognize this or that structure as a plant, if they were not all formed in accordance with one pattern?"[27]

Thus it was probably in Sicily in the spring that he "discovered" the *Urpflanze,* by an act of resignation. Does the plant kingdom really contain individuals? Is there not in this great sea of forms one plant *part* which prefigures not only the entire plant but all possibilities of plant development?

> Tell Herder that I am very close to the secret of the generation and organization of plants and that it is the simplest imaginable. One can make the most delightful observations beneath this sky! Tell him that I have discovered quite clearly and beyond any question the main point, where the germ lies hidden, and that I already have an overview of the whole thing, and only a few points still need to be worked out. The *Urpflanze* is becoming the most curious creation in the world, and even nature will envy me. He who once has this pattern and the key to it can

invent an infinite number of plants which have to be consistent, that is, even if they do not exist, they could exist, and not as picturesque or poetic shades and fancies, but possessed of an inner truth and necessity. The same law will prove applicable to everything else.[28]

Whereas the archetypal stone, granite, was a natural phenomenon, it is clear that the archetypal plant is not to be found in nature: it is Goethe's own perception, which she will "envy" him.

He continued to occupy himself with these speculations during the summer and fall, even speaking of his proposed "Harmonia Plantarum, which will illuminate the Linnean system in the most delightful way, resolve all points of contention about plant forms, even explain all deformities."[29] Botany, however, is a study which cannot be pursued well in an artist's atelier on the Corso, and the execution of this ambitious plan was postponed until after the return to Weimar. By the time Goethe actually set about writing, he had at last hit upon the correct title, a word which biologists in many other fields have envied him, *morphology.*

Thus he was able to state his major contention in the title, *Morphology of Plants*[30] — that the fundamental problem of the biologist is to explain how organic forms come about, how one structure develops, specializes, gives rise to another. Goethe demonstrates how the plant leaf adapts itself so as to form chalice, calyx, and other blossom parts, calling attention for emphasis to deformities in which the blossom reverts again to the production of leaves. He goes so far as to view the seed capsule as a variant of leaf structure; indeed, he asserts that the entire plant is, fundamentally, a leaf. Although his early notes from Italy mention stem and root parts as also prefigured in the leaf, the *Morphology of Plants* tends rather to ignore them.

Goethe appears to have fallen victim to the same kind of error which he had so frequently deplored in others. He chided his friend Knebel, for example, in the following words. "Drawing distinctions is more difficult and tedious than finding similarities. ... Once you begin to find things identical or similar you are prone, in behalf of your hypothesis or your viewpoint, to overlook ways in which things differ greatly."[31] Even more to the point had been his admonition to Philipp Seidel to "think less highly of your opinion than of your eye." But there is no question that Goethe had by middle age become attached to his opinions, especially his scientific ones; the importance of his work in natural history, both in comparative anatomy and in plant morphology, lies less in the specific finding than in the philosophy of nature which led to the finding.

Shortly after publication of the *Morphology of Plants* he wrote to a friend: "In the same manner, on the same path as my botanical essay I am continuing my observations in all the kingdoms of nature and applying all the tricks I know to come closer to the general laws in accordance with which living beings organize themselves."[32] We have observed how he felt the most important general law of the organism to be the perfect interrelationship of its parts. Hence he insisted that the understanding of any specific organ lay in a study of all the rest, for the development and continuance of any one depends on a delicate balance among them all. He was sure he could extend this same principle through the entire plant and animal kingdom, and his attempt to do so made him one of the very early researchers in ecology. The following sketches reveal the pattern of his thinking:

> Thus we shall proceed in this line of study and, as we are just now learning to regard unorganized, indeterminate elements as the seedbed of anorganic compounds, we shall in the future advance our observations and regard the organic world as a context of many elements. The entire plant kingdom, for example, will appear to us as another tremendous sea which is just as necessary for the conditioned existence of the insects as the

oceans and rivers for the conditioned existence of the fish, and we shall see that a tremendous number of living creatures are born and nourished in this plant sea, indeed we shall finally regard the entire animal world only as another great element where one race has its continuation in and from the other, if not its very origin. We shall accustom ourselves to regard relationships and connections as something other than predetermined or purposeful, and in this way alone shall we make progress in understanding how formative nature everywhere manifests herself. And our experience will convince us . . . that the most palpable and extensive utility for mankind is the result only of great unselfish efforts which do not, like a day-laborer, demand their pay at the end of the week, and need not even show their usefulness for humanity at the end of a decade or a century.[33]

Goethe was unable to view nature except in context. Unfortunately, his was not a way of thinking shared by science during the nineteenth century. This Goethean mode of perception recommends itself mainly by its comprehensiveness — we get the feeling that such a general overview must be valid if only because it is not self-contradictory. In any case it forbids specialization, because any one field of study relies on many others for its meaning. This appears to be the red thread which marks each of Goethe's attempts at serious thinking: artistic composition, politics, natural history, art history. In each he is striving for a synthetic overview of a wide range of data as a harmonious entirety. So long as the "professional scholars" believed in absolute advancement of their several fields by the successive displacement of one model by a better one, Goethe's work in any one of their specialties tended to be judged in terms of whatever model of nature happened to be current. The development of the history of science may have limited our confidence in scientific progress, but in return it has permitted us a better appreciation of one individual scientist's views as not really the less valid from a humane standpoint, even when they are superseded by the narrower interests of the scientific community.

NOTES

1. Bodmer to Schinz on May 28, 1776. Grumach 1, 418.
2. *Betrachtungen im Sinne der Wanderer. JA* 39, 72.
3. *Vorwort zur Morphologie. JA* 39, 251.
4. To Carl August on November 4, 1781.
5. To Merck on April 8, 1785.
6. Schiller to Körner on August 12, 1787. Herwig, 397.
7. December 21, 1787.
8. March 27, 1784.
9. To Knebel on November 17, 1784.
10. *Schema vergleichender Osteologie. LA* 9, 121.
11. Ibid., p. 125.
12. Ibid., pp. 135 f.
13. July 6, 1780. Grumach II, 248 f.
14. October 11, 1780.
15. To Charlotte on August 16, 1786.
16. December 27, 1780.
17. October 27, 1782.
18. June 20, 1784.
19. To Charlotte on October 5, 1784.
20. Theorie der Gesteinlagerung. *LA* 1, 96 f.
21. December 20, 1784.
22. To Merck on April 8, 1785.
23. *Geschichte meines botanischen Studiums. JA* 39, 302.
24. Ibid., *LA* 9, 16.
25. Diary, September 27, 1786.
26. To Charlotte on February 19, 1787.
27. April 17, 1787.
28. To Charlotte on June 8, 1787.
29. To Knebel on August 18, 1787.
30. Published in 1790.
31. *Kristallisation und Vegetation. JA* 39, 10.
32. To Jakobi on March 20, 1791.
33. *Versuch einer allgemeinen Vergleichungslehre. LA* 10, 122.

Niedere Minne

W E are exceptionally well in-
formed about the trip down to Rome in the fall of 1786. We
have Goethe's detailed travel diary for the Lady Charlotte, as
well as the *Italian Journey* as he compiled it in his late sixties. It
often fills out the contemporary reports with additional recollections, and its accuracy is, in turn, generally borne out by the
contemporary records. We also have a fairly extensive correspondence from the fall. Subsequent months are much less well docu-
mented. Goethe neglected his diary. The *Italian Journey* for the
year 1787 was therefore very dependent on surviving letters, and
Goethe mutilated them in the process of writing it. The first
months of the year are so eventful that we do not feel we have
lost track of his activities, and we may forget that we have become
entirely dependent on the much older Goethe and what he chose
to communicate about his excursion to Naples and Sicily. Virtually no letters survive. The last extant love letter to Charlotte
comes down to us because, after finishing the *Italian Journey* in
1818, Goethe gave it to a friend, calling it "an ancient leaf which
I could not burn when I dedicated all the papers relative
to Naples and Sicily to the fire. It is such a nice commentary on
the turning point of the whole adventure, casting a glow back-
wards and forwards. It is yours! Take good care of it. How sweet
we are when we are young."[1]

His tendency in the *Italian Journey* to depersonalize the papers as he incorporated and destroyed them makes it extremely difficult for us to gain an immediate and vivid image of his residence in Rome after he settled there in the summer of 1787. Certain episodes do stand out sharply, but close scrutiny can seldom penetrate their veil of poetry. His visit to a wealthy art dealer at Castel Gondolfo in October, for example, is blurred in soft fall colors. Here he says he met and became enamored of a charming patrician from Milan — like Lotte in Wetzlar, already engaged and inaccessible. We would be so grateful for one confirming scrap of paper preserving the slightest direct reference to his meeting with the fair Milanese. We have only the much older man's reflection, presented as such, with delicacy and art.

Most Goethe biographers are convinced that he took a mistress during his stay in Rome, their main evidence being a cycle of elegies which he may have written there, and which we shall describe in detail at the end of this chapter. Some have actually thought that they could extract her name and address — a young widow with a child, daughter of an *osteria* owner near the Theater of Marcellus — but they are wrong. Whether he had a mistress and who she was is a mystery. Nevertheless, precisely such imponderables as this may give us a better feeling for a person's life and character than can the so-called facts. We shall address ourselves therefore to the general problem of love in Goethe's life, knowing that we shall raise more questions than answers.

Carl August's sex life was anything but enigmatic. His promiscuity may have been partly caused by the coldness of his duchess; certainly it contributed to her neuroses. Still, such behavior was probably expected of the lord of the land. In a jovial way he encouraged Goethe to follow his example, although he entertained no real hope of overcoming the gentle but austere power of the Lady Charlotte. Once Goethe was down in Italy, Carl August's good-natured prompting became more sanguine. But still Goethe regarded overnight affairs as out of the question, and as to more serious liaisons, the following letter to Carl August from Rome probably answers any questions we might have: "Here as everywhere you cannot become involved with the fairer sex without loss of time. The girls, or rather the young women who sit as models for the painters, are very sweet, and they are willing to be looked at, and enjoyed. It would be a very convenient pleasure if the French influences did not make this paradise, too, uncertain. I will bring home the portrait of one of these creatures. You've never seen anything more delicate."[2] Fear of the "French disease" was so profound in Goethe as to make us doubt that he took Carl August's suggestions very seriously, despite the fact that the duke seems even to have provided a prophylactic formula which Goethe promised to use once he got to Naples. Goethe had a most remarkable ability to accommodate tone and content of his letters to the mentality of the recipient, and he had especially good reason to use this talent in the duke's case. He was continuing Goethe's full salary for the Italian trip, and Goethe was eager for him to know how well it was agreeing with him. If Carl August was not likely to conceive of a pleasant trip without sexual adventures, why should one quibble on a matter of taste and risk causing Carl August to miss the real point: that he was enjoying himself immensely, in his own way?

When, in January, Goethe raised the question with his Weimar friends as to whether he should venture on from Naples to Sicily, Carl August generously responded that he need not plan to return home before winter. Still, Goethe did not seriously consider extending his absence much beyond the summer of 1787. When he arrived back from Sicily in May, he was fully planning on a prompt departure for Germany and looking forward to celebrating his birthday (28 August) in Frankfurt. He told Charlotte not to write to him in Rome anymore: "I really long to be home. I also want to gather up, in a quiet and unassuming manner, whatever awaits me along the way. If I find the peace I seek you will all see what I have gained. Everything that bespeaks your love is infinitely dear to me, even your sorrowful notes, now that you have regained your composure."[3] The last reference is to her earlier indignation at his long silence.

He wrote also to Carl August about business matters, because he hoped to prepare a different role for himself in Weimar. The presidency of the Chamber, he asked, should be formally transferred to the competent member of the Council who was functioning in Goethe's absence. For the rest, he wished to retain only those duties which he alone could perform. His tone is very persuasive: "My relationship with official duties arose from my relationship to you; let now a new relationship to you displace the official one. . . . I can already tell what a help the trip has been, how it has enlightened me and brightened my existence. As you have borne me up thus far, continue to care for me. You will do me more good than I myself can, more than I could wish, or ask. Give me back to myself, to my country, give me back to yourself, so that I may begin a new life, and a new way of living with you."[4] This letter, like the one to Charlotte, is from Naples.

His plans for return were obviously firm, but he was scarcely back in Rome before they began to waver. We can only guess at the reason, and it may be that all our guesses would be right. If he was to withdraw from official capacities, was it not a good idea to give those concerned, especially his former subordinate, the new President of the Chamber, time to accustom themselves to the change? And if he was to devote himself primarily to art and to his studies, was there really much urgency about withdrawing to Weimar? As he observed to Charlotte only two days after arriving in Rome: "I must concentrate my efforts on the last four volumes. . . . Where I go about it, here or in Frankfurt, makes no difference, and Rome is the only place in the world for the artist — I am, after all, nothing else. If the return trip in winter, or near winter, just weren't so difficult."[5]

Resuming his lodging on the Corso must have struck him as something of a homecoming after three months of traveling. He had a deep affection for the city, certain that it still held a wealth of material with value for his entire life, and he feared he would never return. June alone did not really suffice for making all final arrangements and saying all the farewells. The celebrated painter Hackert accompanied him in return visits to especially beloved spots, then persuaded him to take out two weeks in Tivoli. If he would only stay over in Rome for eighteen months, Hackert promised, he would make a genuine artist of him. When Goethe came back to the rooms on the Corso toward the end of June, he found them a real oasis from the heat. With the ebullient and sometimes difficult Tischbein off to Naples again, the spacious quarters (including an enviable studio with superb lighting) were left entirely at Goethe's disposal. Who is to say which of these considerations finally determined him to celebrate his thirty-eighth birthday not in the city of his birth, but in that of his re-birth? In typical fashion, he claimed that Carl August was responsible:

> Hail, health, and best wishes first of all, wherever this letter may find you. Your blessing, your admonition has borne fruit now. For the first time on my entire trip I have the genuine feeling of *sodezz*, in Rome where *sodezz*, or extreme frivolity, is at home. . . . I am more diligent day by day and pursue art, which is such a serious matter, more and more seriously. If I could only overcome a few problems in technique! In the con-ception, in true, immediate conception, I am far out ahead. Since I am, after all, an artist, it will contribute a great deal to my happiness and to my future light-hearted existence at home if my little talent does not always have to crawl and scrawl

along, but can work with a free spirit — if only as an amateur.
I am indebted to you also for what I am learning right now,
because without your kind encouragement . . . I would have left
Rome by now.[6]

The opening of that letter may incline us to accept as autobiographical a passage in Goethe's *Roman Elegies* where the poet
insinuates that he has taken a mistress in compliance with his
lord's advice.[7] Certainly if Goethe did at any time in Rome have
a mistress — and there is good reason to doubt that he did —
then these summer months appear to be the most likely ones. We
know little more, however, than that he spent the heat of the
day in his relatively cool rooms perfecting drawing techniques,
doing some figure studies, venturing occasionally out into the sun
to try a landscape, working from time to time on *Egmont*. On
some evenings he was attracted down into the streets, where life
began only after dark. There had been a time when he would
have been quite incapable of striking up an easy acquaintance,
let us say at an *osteria*, or of arranging there for a rendezvous
elsewhere, as he depicts in the *Roman Elegies*. Had his outlook
and bearing changed sufficiently to permit it now?

Our strongest positive indication comes not from Rome, but
from Weimar, where the Lady Charlotte sensed a change in him,
and was offended by it. She was familiar with *Egmont* as Goethe
had brought it with him from Frankfurt in 1775. He had worked
on it during the years when his devotion to her was at its poetic
and mystical peak, tried but failed to attack the problem in Rome
before Sicily, and at last succeeded in completing the drama after
his return to the city. He mailed it off to Weimar in August and,
in his usual eagerness, soon began asking if his friends had read
it and how they liked it. At first the Lady appears to have replied in general terms, mostly approving but finding some fault
in the characterization of Clara, the heroine. She expressed her
disapproval with such a harsh phrase that Goethe inquired fur-

ther, whereupon she admitted that the drama was causing her "more pain than pleasure."[8]

This is one of those instances where we may be astonished at Goethe's obtuseness, masculine insensitivity, or simply boyish thoughtlessness. His reply went something like this: "Oh it is clear enough that such an extensive composition can scarcely acquire an entirely pure tone. At basis no one but the artist himself has a true concept of the difficulty of art."[9] He continued into more abstract aesthetic reflections, but his denial of a creation "entirely pure" was in itself a refutation of the Lady Charlotte's most fundamental teachings. Her objection, furthermore, had not been on grounds of art at all, but of character. She had not been able to reconcile herself, she said, to a heroine who appeared now as a goddess, and now as a whore.[10]

Clara, the beloved of Egmont, is a young woman of the middle or lower class who lives alone with her mother. In this and in a few other details she resembles the mistress* of the *Roman Elegies*. She spurns the prospects of a good marriage to accept clandestine visits from her dashing nobleman. He usually comes cloaked as one of the folk, but the drama depicts the single night when he accedes to her request that he wear his splendid foreign court uniform. The mother, who in vanity encouraged the relationship at first, now troubles herself about the future, but Clara, in the complete devotion typical of Goethe's women, shows no trace of care. When Egmont's life is endangered by the regime, she flies out onto the streets seeking to foment a revolution to save him. In Act V Egmont, having resigned himself to his execution, recommends Clara to the love of a Spanish nobleman in order to assure her security. All the ladies in Weimar objected to this stroke.

Charlotte's unusually harsh objection appears to have been to the final scene, where Egmont is sleeping soundly and dreaming — we see the vision on stage — of the Goddess Freedom leading his Dutch folk to independence. The Lady may have been familiar with the vision itself. New to her, obviously, was the necessity of reconciling this goddess with a "whore," for in the finished *Egmont* Freedom appears in the figure of Clara. Although Goethe had mentioned *Egmont* fairly often to Charlotte while working on it in Weimar, Clara's name does not come up in those years at all. We do find reference in his letters to the other feminine role, Margaret of Parma. She is a mature woman who, as regent of the Netherlands, must contend against the youthful and willful Egmont, but at the same time holds an unspoken, strong affection for him and wishes to temper his extravagant, dangerous ways. To the extent that the relationship between Margaret and Egmont matches that at the time between Charlotte and Goethe, we are inclined to think that the heroine of this early *Egmont* may not have been Clara. If Clara figured in this version at all, perhaps she and her fiance were involved in some kind of Shakespearean subplot which the Lady Charlotte found unobjectionable. She did not reject Faust's Gretchen, for example, who was punished horribly for going astray. It seems improbable that Clara, if she yielded herself to Egmont in the play as Charlotte knew it, did so with impunity, and certainly she did not turn up as a goddess in the end. Least of all did Egmont confide to her that Margaret of Parma "has a little moustache and sometimes an attack of gout. A real Amazon." These are surely among the new lines which caused Charlotte "more pain than pleasure."

Egmont was the last major work to be completed in Italy. In the same days in which it was receiving its final touches its author decided for some reason not to leave Rome at all that summer, but, for the time being, to continue his residence there. Since we have so little direct knowledge of his life and associations at the time, any inferences we might wish to make from *Egmont* are the purest conjecture. Definite is only that in August he made formal request of Carl August that he be permitted to remain in Rome until Easter.

His enthusiasm about Italy had the ironic side effect of creating a disturbing amount of interest among Weimaraners. Goethe recalled in the *Italian Journey* how "at last the dam broke, it gradually becoming apparent that, on the one hand the Dowager Duchess and her entourage, on the other hand Herder and the younger Dalberg were making serious preparations to cross the Alps. My advice was that they should wait until the winter was over and arrive in Rome in the temperate season" — or after he was gone.[11] He offered numerous authoritative reasons to substantiate his good advice,[12] but admitted in the *Italian Journey* that his major consideration was an understandable aversion to being drawn into a circle of German tourists. The upshot was also ironic. The old duchess accepted Goethe's friendly suggestions and asked that her son command him to wait on her in Italy the next spring.

This news arrived in early 1788, and the eagerness which he now showed to get out of Rome is truly remarkable. His letter to Carl August is probably their longest single piece of correspondence. First a clear, itemized statement of all the personal and artistic considerations which had motivated his trip to Italy in the first place, then a conscientious account of his accomplishments there, month by month, a projection also for the coming months and his reasons for returning by Easter. "If, however, your will keeps me here to serve the Lady your mother, then I shall from Easter forward begin a new life in order to qualify myself for the post of Tour Marshall. I take out a new page in order to present my plans for your approval." He explains how his purposes hitherto have required avoidance of high society, "for the world does not give, but takes, and my aversion to half-way measures increases daily." Now, however, he will acquire the proper accoutrements, engage a domestic, furnish his rooms appropriately, wait on the members of temporal and Church government (he itemizes them), and do all those other things expected of a courtier. He assures his patron in unctuous tones that no one can look after such matters better than he, nor are the duchess and her company likely to find a more competent guide to the art treasures of Italy. His preparations in Rome alone will consume the month of April; May he will devote to the same efforts in Naples. Thus, when the duchess arrives, he will not be ashamed to take charge of all her affairs, dealing with the natives himself, lest she or her court be compromised or cheated. He goes into detail about how he will accomplish these duties, yet he promises to undertake none of them until Carl August confirms his command: "Then I shall regard myself as a servant of the duchess and subordinate the remainder of my existence to this obligation."[13]

Obviously, he was anxious to keep his life in Rome quite separate from his relationships to Weimar. Yet if we take this as an indication of a love affair there, then his willingness, even eagerness, to leave by Easter would also have to be explained. When, as was to be expected, Carl August wrote that he and his mother were sure that Goethe had more to lose from attending her in Italy than she stood to gain, Goethe's reply was not without emotion: "I answer your kind, cordial letter immediately with a joyful: I come! This fulfills my hopes, my wishes, my first intentions."[14] If there had been any serious attachment in the summer of 1787, it no longer held him by the spring of 1788. As a matter of fact, he responded to Carl August's somewhat lurid descriptions of his own sexual exploits by pointing out the extreme difficulties and dangers which attended such adventures in Rome and concluded with the decisive statement: "In so far as the heart is concerned, the word is not even in the vocabulary of the Italian Chancellery of love."[15]

Still, Charlotte's uneasy feeling that some sort of turning point in Goethe's interests and outlook was occurring during the Roman residence tends to be confirmed by that lengthy account rendered Carl August. The *Italian Journey* of August, 1787, is more emphatic, stating that once the decision to stay in Rome had been made, "a period of a new kind began." "I am doing fine in body and soul and can almost hope for a radical cure. Everything I try is easy, and sometimes there comes a breath from the time of my youth."[16] Such testimony corresponds with his remark to Herder that he had been, for the first time in his life, absolutely happy.[17]

He still made no formal debut in society after settling down in Rome, but he no longer avoided contacts, either. His declared purpose for the incognito of the previous winter had been to conserve time. Now he seems to have all the time in the world, and he squanders it. Daily among lighthearted friends, he spends long hours in the cool of the Sistine Chapel, dozes there in the Pope's chair. Weeks at a time are spent exploring the environs of Rome. He squanders money, too, living quite simply but spending readily on his friends and perhaps, like the poet of the *Roman Elegies,* on a mistress as well. His entire Weimar salary is consumed, as well as the unreasonably high honorarium for his first four volumes (one thousand talers). Progress with the last four is minimal. "One likes to spend the whole day sketching and drawing, and mornings and evenings there is so much to do just keeping the sheets in order, shading in the contours or inking in the outlines. And one dabbles a bit in oils, and the time gets away just as if that's the way it had to be."[18] Although he claims to be very aware of his un-Roman outlook, in that he can view the people more critically than ever before, he certainly seems to have forfeited Northern diligence and conscientiousness. He no longer thinks of himself as a German author in the traditional sense, but wishes to write an *opera buffa.* The Necklace Affair, he thinks, can be well adapted to this form.

In Weimar he had collaborated with his boyhood friend Philipp Kayser in an operetta, and now he was interested in continuing that relationship. A copy of *Egmont* went to Kayser so that he could provide music for the Freedom Vision of Act V, and he planned to visit Kayser in Zurich on his return trip. His main interest in literature appears now to have been in context with music, and when the trip through Switzerland was postponed, he persuaded Kayser to join him in Rome. He lived with Goethe from November until both returned to Zurich in the spring. They worked on the operettas which were to fill out Volume V — the Egmont volume. The light-hearted, noncommittal tone of the pieces can be taken as a fair reflection of Goethe's own carefree, sociable existence at the time. Both of the little works, *Claudine of Villa Bella* and *Erwin and Elmire,* are set in Italy.

In each operetta two sets of lovers overcome problems of personality and circumstance to be happily united in the end. In *Claudine,* the superior of the two, we can easily perceive Goethe's attachment to Rome; in *Erwin and Elmire* we are tempted to discover how Cupid set his life there in disarray. Nevertheless, both operettas, like the composer Kayser himself, go back a dozen years to Goethe's Frankfurt time of social gadding, music, and pretty girls in bright parlors. Compared with the finesse and luster of the Italian versions, to be sure, the Frankfurt prototypes appear awkward indeed.

In each of the early versions there was only one pair of lovers, and *Claudine* even brought a male lead whom the plot left dangling, if not forgetting about him, at least embarrassed by him. This is Crugantino, a brash and rebellious young fellow who refuses to reconcile himself with society. Such sentiments as his were clearly out of place in a genre like the operetta, which aims solely at light entertainment and adornment of the status quo. When the fortunate lovers are delivered into each others' arms and he, the odd rebel, is admonished to behave himself better, he snaps:

With your permission, Sir, you don't know what you are talking about. What do you mean "behave"? Do you know the needs of a young heart, of a mad young head? Where is there a place for me in your way of life? I find your middle-class society unbearable. If I want to work, I must be a lackey; if I want to play, I must be a lackey. Will not anyone who is half a man prefer the open spaces? — Pardon me. I do not like to hear other people's opinions. Pardon me for speaking mine. To make up for it I will grant you that anyone who once begins an undisciplined existence soon knows no limits and accepts no restrictions, for our heart, alas, is boundless so long as its strength holds out.

Crugantino's sentiments from the spring of 1775 may be very important in our speculations about Goethe's love life in later years. In that same spring he came closest to getting married and taking up his proper, middle-class place in Frankfurt social and professional circles. His inability to reconcile himself to it is what allowed for the poignant relationships of later years. Here is no longer the place to explore Crugantino's "boundless heart" or his "mad young head"; their implications are clear enough in Werther. We shall, however, pause long enough to tell the story of how Goethe, too, like any other young Frankfurt lad of good family, was once engaged to a fine young lady — perhaps a bit too fine.

While his mother did come from an old established house, his father's people were only second generation, real upstarts from the patricians' point of view — and neither side counted among Frankfurt's really wealthy set. Lili's mother, on the other hand, came from the so-called patrician class, related to the medieval rulers of the city, and her father was a rich financier. Her family, the Schönemanns, also belonged to a somewhat exclusive Calvinist minority, while Goethe's parents were Lutheran. The two families were strangers with nothing in common, pursuing entirely different lifestyles. It was only because Wolfgang Goethe, as darling of the young intellectuals, had acquaintances over a wide range of social sectors that he happened to accompany a group to a party at the Schönemann house. Thus the stunning author in his brown coat and cravat found himself standing at the piano in a brightly lighted parlor, quite taken by the delicate blond pianist, his hostess Lili.

Their attraction to one another lent the spring of 1775 a special character. Most of Wolfgang's free time was spent with Lili. They made frequent visits to a composer friend of hers in nearby Offenbach, and it was probably in this way that Goethe was encouraged to try his own operettas — more, incidentally, than those that survive. His quick gift of language and wit could turn an ordinary event — as when she was late for her birthday party — into a facile little genre piece. This was one of his most productive but least successful periods. He tried to write an obscene farce, of which only the outrageous *dramatis personae* and a few fragments survive. There is a remarkable little drama, *Stella,* where the hero, married to a good, loving *Hausfrau,* meets and falls in love with a charming and intelligent, in every way more attractive woman. He marries her, too, and in the end his wives embrace in happy accord. *Stella* is not entirely incongruous with Goethe's own situation. Indeed, it may point up the major importance of the Lili affair for his future.

His parents had already recognized that the time was overripe for their son to bring a wife home, establish the usual connections, and make sensible provisions for the family to continue in its solid, middle-class way for another generation. In routine fashion a suitable party had been found, Goethe had behaved complacently, and discussions had begun with the girl's parents.[19] In due course all would reach the usual consummation. His mother was already looking to the linens and wondering if the family cradle would be serviceable for another brood. No one really expected the young man to show any ardor — a sensible marriage was not an affair of the heart — all that was required of him was courtesy and cooperation. All went smoothly until the Lili affair. There could be no question of continuing nuptial plans when the groom was so obviously smitten with another girl. But the family thinking had a kind of inexorable logic to it. Here was a son in his middle twenties; he had a promising law practice which was suffering only from his distractions and expensive entertainment of literary admirers. The solution was obvious, and if it turned out to involve a young woman for whom he held some spontaneous affection, so much the better. Within an astonishingly short span of time the earlier arrangements had been dismissed and, with the aid of relatives, a formal engagement with Lili materialized by Easter. The Calvinist community immediately began a conspiracy against the alliance.

The young couple themselves were a little surprised at what had happened to them. However fond they were of one another, they seem to have known from the outset that an engagement was not very realistic. When all was said and done, she would have to surrender an enviable position in Frankfurt's influential circles, where she had been spoiled by young and old, for a comfortable but humdrum life in the house of Goethe's parents. He placed his dearest hopes in an escape from Frankfurt. Accomplishing it would entail insecurity and perhaps an even more unsatisfactory life for a spouse, unless marriage actually held him at home, living with his father and engaged as junior partner in his father-in-law's banking enterprise. The engagement meant a decisive turning point in the love affair. Within three weeks he accepted the invitation of two young counts, admirers of *Götz* and *Werther,* to accompany them to Switzerland. On the way he visited his melancholy sister in the remote little town of Emmendingen. Wretched in her own marriage and unable to imagine a more fortunate situation than Lili's single state, she urged her brother not to wed this girl to unhappiness.

In Zurich he met friends from Frankfurt, including Philipp Kayser. With some of them he crossed Lake Zurich and then hiked south to the Gotthard. He recalled being tempted to continue on to Italy, but felt that it was the bond to Lili that drew him back. Some of his most touching love lyrics are those written to her in this summer. They lend credence to his later statement that it was his first and only great love. In any case, the trip served its purpose. When he arrived home at the end of July, all concerned were resigned to the realities of the situation, which became final, of course, with his invitation to Weimar. This is the way it came about that Goethe, when caught between two women, did not, like the hero of his drama, marry both of them. His engagement to a girl whom he deeply loved broke off realistic prospects of a commonsense marriage and became the main reason for his failure to marry at all.

We can best appreciate the powerful influence of the Lady Charlotte by reflecting that he showed little normal interest in women during the ten years in her *Minnedienst*. He was the darling of the ladies at court, and at neighboring courts as well. His garden house on the Ilm was a favorite retreat in nice weather for the exceptionally beautiful Corona Schröter, the idol of his teens, who invariably came with one or more of her young lady friends or, for a time, with the duke — Carl August's hopes of a conquest rose at one time so high that the duchess banned the chaste Corona from court — and there were other young ladies with other affairs, but none seem in any way to have affected Goethe directly, although he remained the favorite of them all.

How different was their attitude toward him when he returned from Italy in the spring of 1788! And how different his own attitude toward their daughters! One of his closest friends, Charlotte's sister, was deeply disturbed "that at the lawn party yesterday he had almost nothing to say to any of the intelligent ladies, but kissed the hands of all the girls, flirted with them and danced a lot. The Lady von Kalb was horrified to see him excite the young things in this way."[20] Already from letters written while on his way home we can note his natural concern about whether his friends are going to find him changed. He fears that, from their point of view, he is going to appear "terribly uncivilized."[21] His very dress betrayed him. He still wore his conservative brown — always his favorite color — but his shoes now bore brightly jeweled buckles,[22] something which surely must have struck the Lady Charlotte as appropriate only for a young fop or an old roué. And she no doubt told him so. "I will be by for a moment this morning," so goes the first surviving note to her. "I am happy to hear whatever you have to say to me. I must only ask that you not be too severe with my somewhat uncomposed, if not distraught condition. I can assure you that my inner state is not the same as my outer appearance."[23]

It seems likely that he at first underestimated the distance which had come to separate him from his old friends. In his typical openness, especially with Charlotte, his first impulse was to confide his most important recent experiences. Her extremely unsympathetic response leads us to think that he may have made the mistake of telling her about a love affair in Italy. "I won't mention again what I left behind in Italy. You received my confidence on that subject unkindly enough."[24] By the time that this remark was made, almost a year after his return, the relationship to Charlotte had greatly deteriorated. We shall have to postpone consideration of their falling out until another chapter, because it belongs with the other difficulties which he encountered in adjusting to his new life at home. Here we wish to pursue the question of sexual love, a part of his life from which Charlotte had early excluded herself. Perhaps she had not understood that her feelings for him did go beyond the platonic, but she may have come to know herself better in this regard after his return. Caroline Herder reported to her husband: "I have from Stein herself the secret now of why she is no longer on good terms with Goethe. He has the young Vulpius girl as his Clara, has her at his house often, etc. She resents this and feels that since he is such an exceptional person, and a forty-year-old man [not quite — he had just turned thirty-nine] he should not do anything which reduces him to a common level."[25]

Christiane Vulpius was a twenty-three-year-old girl from Weimar's poverty-stricken middle class. She worked in the new artificial flower factory run by Bertuch, the businessman who was involved in the venture of publishing Goethe's works. The edition had, by the time of Goethe's return in June, 1788, progressed only through Volume V, and Goethe no doubt called on Bertuch fairly soon after his arrival. It may have been in this way that he came upon Christiane. Weimar legend has it that it was she who approached him, seeking patronage for her brother. However that may be, her age and situation no longer permitted her the prospect of a very good marriage. She was a down-to-earth girl, by no means bashful, and well accustomed to making eyes at attractive men. For his part, Goethe had obviously left many of his inhibitions behind him. We have reason to believe that just a little over three weeks after he arrived in Weimar Christiane spent her first night in his cottage.

The couple was discreet, so that several months passed before the relationship became a topic for gossip. Most people found it easy enough to accept at the time, but later generations, with their changed social assumptions, had more difficulty appreciating Christiane's capacity first as Goethe's mistress, later as his housekeeper. His touching request, for example, that Charlotte help maintain their old confidence lest the Christiane affair "degenerate" into a more serious relationship occurred at a time when his mistress was over two months pregnant.[26] Even when their son was a year old, he seriously considered entering into a marriage which would have corresponded with his social position.[27] The liaison with Christiane was on a purely sensual level, and may have even occurred as a kind of reaction to and release from the Weimar environment, where for so many years he had sublimated his drives in devotion to work and to the Lady Charlotte. It may also have been a final glimmering reflection of experiences in Italy.

The affair had gone on for a little over three months when Goethe enclosed a so-called *Erotikon* in a letter to a friend.[28] This is the first we hear of what became the *Roman Elegies*, his most sensual and perhaps his most beautiful love lyrics. We know that many of them were written over the next eighteen months. He began to concern himself seriously with Propertius, whose erotic poetry serves as a kind of model for some of the *Elegies*, only after he returned from Italy. Thus we might have some reason to suppose that the remarkably intimate scenes depicted in them all derive from his bed with Christiane. Indeed, from time to time he called her his little *Erotikon*. Yet, when he mentioned the poems to his publisher, he referred to "a little book of elegies I wrote in Rome."[29] We know, of course, that this is not entirely true, but is it partially correct? The manuscript itself bears the title *Erotica Romana. Rome 1788.* Did he actually begin them there perhaps, and do they deal with an attachment in Rome? Or were they all written later and given this title because they reflect earlier Roman experiences — or at least a state of mind in Rome, and his daydreams there? We have no answer to such questions, because Goethe himself disposed of most of the direct documentation of his Roman sojourn. Clearly, the *Roman Elegies,* like the operettas revised there, and like *Egmont,* must themselves be included among our scanty records. We will outline them here and encourage the reader to make his own assessment of their autobiographical significance.

The meter is new for Goethe, classical hexameters. Many motifs are classical as well, while the costume is modern. The content, elegy by elegy, is as follows.

I. A stranger enters Rome, whose stones, palaces and streets are as yet mute:

> Who will tell me in whispers, where will I find the window
> Where someday I'll glimpse the dear creature who'll scorch me with
> love.
> Can I not yet divine the paths through which over and over
> To her and from her I'll go, squandering my valuable time?

For the present he wisely views the sights, knowing that Rome won't be Rome without love.

II. He scorns to enter grand palaces and their splendor. A coarse woolen dress is removed more readily than brocade and fishbone, and the creaking of a simple bed is a pleasant sound.[30]

III. He has escaped the lords and ladies who incessantly ask about *Werther*. His beloved scarcely knows his name, and associates it only with a strange land.[31]

IV. She ought not regret having yielded herself so readily — this is one of the Propertian motifs — for the gods make love spontaneously, and thus were Rome's founders conceived.

V. Among the many gods honored in Rome, the lovers most mischievously and assiduously celebrate the Goddess Opportunity.

> Once she appeared to me, too, a dark-skinned girl. Tumbling
> Over her forehead hair in waves heavy and dark,
> Round her delicate neck, short little ringlets
> Unbraided hair curled all up from the crown of her head
> I did not miss her, seized her as she rushed past. Sweetly
> Embrace and kiss straightway she returned, teaching me how.

VI. He admires the classics by day; they admonish him to continue his studies by night. Spying the curve of her breast, running his hand over her hips brings appreciation for the forms in marble.

> I see with an eye that feels, and I feel with a hand that sees.

They do more than make love; they make intelligent conversation, too. When she falls asleep, he reflects, and

> Poems I have produced often enough in her arms
> And the hexameter's beat I've gently tapped out,
> Hand on her back, with my fingertips counting.

VII. The beloved scolding her lover for calling her untrue is another motif borrowed from Propertius. Goethe clothes it with a great deal of specific detail. She is a widow, suspected by her neighbors because her black dress has been replaced by colorful gifts from her lover. They accuse her of trysts with a cleric, because he comes to her by night in a long dark coat, his hair rounded in back to deceive them. She holds her baby to her breast and charges that man pours out his love with desire.

VIII. The poet is happy in Rome, and the Capitoline Hill* is an Olympus for him.

> May Jupiter suffer me here, and let Hermes later conduct me
> Past Cestius' Tomb* gently to Orcus below.

IX. Upon the beloved's observation that she was not an appealing child, the lover points to the grape blossom, colorless as compared with the fruit.

X. They enjoy the crackling fireside in winter — a scene most difficult to reconcile with Rome.

XI. The great of the earth would envy them their bed.

XII. The artist works his best beneath the images of the ancient Pantheon. Among them,

> It is to Bacchus, the wastrel and dreamer, Cythere
> Lifts up her eyes in desire. Even in marble they're damp.
> His embraces she likes to remember, and she seems to be asking:
> Shouldn't our glorious son be standing here at our side?

Their son is the little monster Priapus, often a garden statue in ancient Rome.

XIII. To my garden of love, welcome, declares the poet, I have arranged it with care — but

> Hypocrites hear me, enervated and prudish wrongdoers,
> Comes one of these to squint out over my garden plot

> Disapproving the pure, the natural fruit, oh chastise
> Him from the rear with the post standing red from out of your hips.

Here is the place where we must note that for a century and a half scholars consistently expurgated the *Roman Elegies*. "Enervated and prudish wrongdoers" even deleted these lines from the comprehensive Weimar edition.[32]

XIV. A song of praise to Priapus, whom sensible men like to look upon, and whom girls and matrons admire.[33]

XV. The ancient festivals of harvest and fertility are recalled. They encourage the participants to observe corresponding rites behind the myrtle bush.

XVI. Cupid is celebrated as inspirer to poetry and great deeds who, at the same time, robs us of the strength and resolve to carry them through.

XVII. Let the shutters be closed and the lamp lighted by day, harbingers of the time when the beloved will come.

XVIII. Another Propertian motif individualized in modern detail. The beloved, with her mother at her uncle's *Osteria*, spills wine on the table so as to catch her lover's eye. She draws in the wine a time of rendezvous, and the poet must mark time now by the sun, overviewer of the ancient as of the modern city.

XIX. Their meeting is thwarted by a scarecrow, whom the lover has taken to be the uncle, persistently working in the garden and blocking his secret pathway.

XX. He hated barking dogs until one announced his beloved's arrival, but now,

> When I hear barking it makes me think always: She's coming.
> Or I remember the time when my expected one came.

XXI. Venereal disease is condemned as that curse which most distinguishes modern life and outlook from that of the ancients.

XXII. The poet, who despises sleeping alone but also fears the diseases which attend promiscuity, is happy to be faithful to one true to him.[34]

XXIII. The tale told by many, including Propertius, as to why Fame hates Cupid. He once made a fool of her favorite, Hercules, and has been playing similar tricks on prominent men to this day.

XXIV. As Midas confided his secret to the earth, and the reeds whispered it to all the world, so the poet entrusts his love to fickle hexameters and pentameters.

Some of this material obviously reflects Weimar situations and mood. We must be very cautious about making inferences about the rest. We might, for example, relate the fear of venereal disease to Italy, and we should be justified in doing so. Yet these very elegies seem to be among the few which we are able to date, for in April, 1789, Goethe wrote to Carl August, then suffering from syphilis, that he was attacking that disease with his hexameters and pentameters. We know that he found a "Clara," as Madame Herder put it, in Weimar, and that several of the elegies are best understood in connection with Christiane. It seems extremely difficult to account for all of them in the same context, but at this point the last of the evidence has been presented. Had Goethe wished his life to be an open book, he might never have retreated to Italy.

NOTES

1. To Zelter on February 16, 1818.
2. February 3, 1787.
3. May 25, 1787.
4. May 29, 1787.
5. June 8, 1787.
6. July 6, 1787. *Sodezza* means "firmness, solidity," not "frivolity."
7. "I am wont to obey when my lord doth command." Actually, "lord" (*Gebieter*) refers to Cupid, but the term seems chosen as a knowing wink to Carl August.
8. *Italienische Reise*, December 8, 1787.
9. Ibid.
10. Ibid., November 3, 1787.

11. Ibid., *Bericht* for October, 1787.
12. To Carl August on November 17, 1787.
13. January 25, 1788.
14. March 17, 1788.
15. December 29, 1787.
16. *Italienische Reise,* September 6, 1787.
17. June 5, 1788.
18. To Schnauss on October 1, 1787.
19. I refer to Susanna Margareta Münch, for whom Goethe wrote *Clavigo.* The affect of this drama and its powerful associations for Goethe are not usually recognized. This is perhaps because he himself treats it so lightly in *Dichtung und Wahrheit, Buch XV.*
20. Caroline Herder to her husband on November 14, 1788. Herwig, 456.
21. To Carl August on May 23, 1788.
22. Döde Schulthess to her sister on June 9, 1788. Herwig, 430.
23. July, 1788.
24. June 1, 1789.
25. March 8, 1789. Herwig, 471.
26. June 8, 1789.
27. Henriette von Lüttwitz.
28. To Jakobi on October 31, 1788.
29. To Göschen on July 4, 1791.
30. Elegy II was deleted by Goethe and preserved with three others in manuscript only, called H⁵¹ by G. von Loeper, their editor for the Weimar edition. I have, in this survey of the *Roman Elegies,* guessed at the position they might have taken in the cycle and included them as II, XIII, XIV, and XXII.
31. Elegy III was radically revised for publication. My summary reflects the original.
32. Conscientious scholarship did, to be sure, later include them in a supplement. As Elegy XIII, I insert the third of those preserved only in H⁵¹. In all, Goethe published twenty elegies. He mentions (in a letter to Schiller on May 12, 1795) only the deletion of "the second and sixteenth." Most scholars seem to assume that the cycle originally consisted of only twenty-two elegies, and that "the second and sixteenth" are the first two of the four which we have in manuscript. I, on the other hand, am assuming that Goethe at one time operated with all twenty-four of the elegies, and I have tried to locate the suppressed four in the cycle thematically. I have the notion that further detective work would turn up evidence to support my arrangement or refute it, but in any case bear out a twenty-four-elegy cycle.
33. Elegy XIV stands second in H⁵¹.
34. Elegy XXII stands last in H⁵¹.

Unrest and Creativity

※

Thendhe fall and winter of 1787
were taken up by friends, and perhaps a mistress, but above all
by drawing, painting, and sculpting. The two operettas for filling
out Volume V of the works were not finished until February,
1788. At that time Goethe reported no change in the sequence
of his projects: "Now almost nothing remains before me but the
hill *Tasso* and the mountain *Faust.* I shall rest neither day nor
night until they are both finished. I have a strange affection for
each of them and, recently, wonderful prospects and hopes. All
these recapitulations of old ideas, this reworking of subjects from
which I had thought myself forever cut off and for which I had
lost almost all feeling, gives me great pleasure. This *summa sum-
marum* of my life provides the courage and joy to turn over a
new leaf."[1] Perhaps work on the operettas had brought intriguing
memories which now encouraged him to delve yet further into
his youth; when he finally got down to work, *Faust,* a very early
project, took precedence over *Tasso,* a drama from later years.
If the testimony from the *Italian Journey* accurately reflects the
situation, he managed to add one scene to *Faust* in the latter half
of February. Again he speaks of a courageous effort:

> I had the courage to survey my three final volumes, and I know
> exactly what I want to do, if the heavens grant me the good
> fortune. It was an eventful week, and in retrospect it seems like

a month. First, the plan of *Faust* was developed, and I hope that this operation will turn out well. Of course it is an entirely different matter, finishing the piece now instead of fifteen years ago, but I don't think it will lose anything by it, particularly since I think I have found the thread again. I also feel confident as concerns the general tone. I have already drawn up a new scene, and if I smoke the paper I don't think anybody would be able to distinguish it from the rest. Now that calm and isolation have returned me to the exact plane of my true existence, it is remarkable how like myself I am, and how little my inner nature has suffered under the years and the events. The old manuscript often gives me pause, when I see it before me. It is the very first version, jotted down in the main scenes without any plan. Now it is so yellow with time, so soiled (the leaves never were bound), so brittle and broken at the edges that it really looks like the fragment of an old codex, and just as my intuition and imagination, in those days, removed me into an earlier world, now I must again revert to a younger time, which I myself have lived through.[2]

What this newly written scene accomplished for *Faust* was really of great significance. The manuscript which he describes contained a content flaw reminiscent of the one Napoleon had found in *Werther:* a youthful imagination had somehow perceived two quite separate plots as essential aspects of the same problem. It is a recognized gift of genius to perceive fundamental similarities in a varied range of human experience, but Goethe often failed to carry such complex insights all the way to a unified form. As a consequence much of his energy had to go into reworking and rounding off early concepts. The first few scenes of *Faust* introduced the traditional Doctor Faustus in a somewhat elevated character, the seasoned scholar who despairs of scholarship and turns to the arcane sciences; the remainder of the work revealed in startling poignancy successive glimpses of a tragic love affair between a simple girl and a devoted youth who was attended by the cynical, ruthless devil, Mephistopheles. Absolutely no transition connected the two plots. In Italy Goethe conceived a colorful combination of dream structures, distorted proverbs, and nonsense language entitled "Witch's Kitchen," in which Faust is given a youth potion. In this way the graying professor of the early scenes can continue as a young rake into the later ones. The drink is an aphrodisiac. Exchanges between the witch and Mephistopheles are coarse and bawdy. Faust loses himself in contemplation of a reclining nude; when he speaks, it is to complain that the surroundings constitute a threat to his sanity.

Like many of Goethe's dramatic conceptions, Faust and Mephistopheles are individualities so closely related that neither can really be conceived without the other, and we are inclined to regard them as two aspects of one personality. Some of the Goethean pairs, like Orestes and Pylades, are complementary, but more often we find them in conflict, and the differences between Faust and Mephistopheles are so violent that we do not hesitate to call them schizophrenic. The *Faust* papers as Goethe worked on them in Rome gave an incomplete account of the meeting between these two main figures. Mephistopheles simply turns up in one of the scenes, and we have no idea how Faust has become involved with him. In later years Goethe spoke of a "great gap," which he eventually managed to fill with the famous pact scenes as we know them today, but in Rome he was not able to attack this problem successfully. He turned back to *Tasso* instead. Here, too, was a far more formidable challenge than he had anticipated, and it would not be met until he had returned to Weimar. When he finally finished *Tasso* in the summer of 1789, he declared that *Faust* would have to be published just the way it was, incomplete — for all he knew it would always remain that way. The title of the work which finally appeared in 1790 was *Faust ein Fragment.* It represented the first great failure in the poet's effort to regain and continue the creative impulses from his youth.

The reason for failure may have lain in the nature of the task itself, for *Faust* drew him deeper into the past than any of the other works did. His first boyish enthusiasm for learning, and its disappointment, the excesses of an adolescent love affair — these two major strands of the Faust-Mephistopheles personality derive from Goethe's first university years in Leipzig, from "shells," as he called them, long since cast off, and rejected. He never did achieve much tolerance for these early years. As a very old man he received through the testament of a boyhood friend some of his own old papers, and commented on them: "Actually, they were ancient, carefully preserved letters, whose aspect could not have been pleasing. Here lay before my eyes leaves from my own hand which expressed only too clearly in what pitiful moral limitations the years of my youth had been passed. The letters from Leipzig were utterly hopeless; I consigned them all to the fire."[3] Such feelings were by no means limited to his old age. He made the following diary entry while still in his twenties: "Cleared things up at home, looked through my papers and burned all my old shells. Other times, other worries. A quiet reflection on my past, on our confusion, urgency, thirst for knowledge when we are young, how we go to such great lengths to find some satisfaction, how I found a special gratification in mysteries and dark, fantastic imaginings. How I made only half-hearted efforts in my studies and then dropped them again, how a kind of humble complacency runs through everything I wrote in those days."[4]

Goethe had experienced a late and protracted adolescence. When he went off to Leipzig just after his sixteenth birthday he was a high-strung, emotionally poorly integrated and unstable child. He had never really been away from home alone, and this three-year period was not to be interrupted by visits to or from his family. He was terribly homesick and, as a consequence, wrote so many long-winded and subjective letters that several managed to survive the later housecleanings and burnings. Most are of the sort which makes the embarrassment of the older man understandable. The boy, long in finding himself, fled from one pose to another. We have a good number of his lyrics, too, all in that coy rococo style which permitted love-making in a powdered periwig. The ardently uncritical acceptance of the fashions of his era, typical of boys this age, runs through all these documents. He planned to be a professor of rhetoric.

Almost all surviving letters from the first two Leipzig years are to his sister. Some are in debonair French, others in a dark English style, but there are occasional resorts to franker German.

> I have fallen from the grace of those whom I used to be permitted to visit, and this is because I followed my father's counsel and do not play cards. Hence I am considered to be a superfluous person in company, with whom the hostess does not know what to do.... For six months I have been invited to no other houses than the Böhmes and the Langens. There is another cause for my not being liked by important people. I have somewhat more taste and aesthetic understanding than our gallant world, and in company I was often unable to avoid revealing the wretchedness of their judgments. Nonetheless, my life is as calm and as content as possible. I have a friend in the tutor of the Count of Lindenau, who is banished from society for precisely the same causes as I.[5]

This was a queer duck in his late twenties, Ernst Wolfgang Behrisch. The friendship with him, of a highly emotional sort which went beyond the usual sentimental excesses of the day, points up the boy's strong need for emotional support. Behrisch's unorthodox ways soon cost his position, and he left for Dresden. This means that we have several of Goethe's letters to him and are, as a consequence, a little better informed about his doings and imaginings during the last year in Leipzig, when he was eighteen. They centered largely on the affections of young women. He observes on one occasion that if a mutual girlfriend should become too virtuous, he would become the devil's advocate and thwart her good resolutions. "Do you know me in this tone, Behrisch? It is the tone of a victorious young gentleman. And that tone from me! It is comical. But without swearing as to what I could do with a girl, I do think that I could sed — how the devil should I call it? Enough Monsieur, what would you expect from your quickest and most diligent pupil?"[6]

Several of the letters to Behrisch take the form of journals, even of hour-to-hour reports. There are, for example, four sheets covering a Tuesday through Saturday in which he describes an exceptionally frenetic period caused by his attachment to the daughter at his boarding house. We do not really learn much about the affair itself, but rather about the terrible distress of an excitable young fellow in the throes of jealousy. He all too obviously toys with and explores the potential of nervous and physical breakdown, and observes at last: "My letter is a good start toward an opus. I have read it through again, and am shocked at myself."[7] It is perhaps Goethe's first experience in becoming a figure in one of his own creations.

The psychological turmoil as described to Behrisch is not, on that account, any less genuine. "I have read my letter through again and would certainly tear it up if I were ashamed to appear before you in my true nature. You will recognize the young man precisely in his violent desire and equally violent revulsion, this raging and ecstasy, and you will pity him. Yesterday the same things made the world a hell for me that make it a heaven today, and it will continue thus until I can no longer experience either." Still, when we observe that the girl in question was three years older than he, and that she became engaged to an established suitor shortly after Goethe left Leipzig, we realize that the situation as he reports it to us probably goes beyond the merely factual to become his own melodramatic vision:

Listen, Behrisch, I can never, I will never forsake the girl, and yet I must leave, I will leave [this is his last semester in Leipzig]. But she shall not be forsaken. If she continues to be, as she is now, *worthy* of me! Behrisch! She shall be taken care of! And yet I shall be so cruel as to rob her of hope. I must do that. For he who gives a girl hope makes her a promise. If she can find a good husband, if she can be happy without me, how pleased I shall be. I know my duty toward her. My hand and my estate belong to her. She shall have everything that I *am able to* give her. Cursed be he who looks to his own needs before he looks to those of the girl whom he has made *wretched*. She shall never feel the pain of knowing me in the arms of another until I have felt the pain of knowing her in the arms of another, and perhaps I will spare her this terrible experience even then.[8]

Here is a boy confused by his own conflicting desires, and poorly acquainted with himself. University life has been dissatisfying for him; his relations with the opposite sex have excited an unusually volatile nature. Robustness was not one of his ideals, and as his health became progressively worse from the winter of 1767-68 on, his nervousness and introspection became more pronounced.

In the last months in Leipzig he found a steadying influence for the first time in his life — and for the last time — in religion. Behrisch's successor as the count's tutor was one of those devout Protestants whose large number and great earnestness in contemplative meetings outside the traditional church framework have won them the title Pietists despite the fact that they were not a sect. They were characterized by informal groups which took strong interest in the psychological depths of the individual member, practiced great openness toward one another about the state of their souls, and interpreted religion in terms of a divine love which brings comfort in emotional distress. After returning home to Frankfurt, Goethe was brought in touch with Pietists there. He presented himself as a lovable boy with a good heart but somehow not completely right with God — oh, by no means in mockery, but in "love and acceptance of religion, openness for the Gospels, sacred respect for the Word. . . . To be sure, all of that does not make me a Christian, but is it within *man's* power to make me one?"[9] A question like that could lead to most revealing and touching hours of discussion.

During his teens Goethe had found no satisfactory outlet for the tensions of an exceptional personality, even though he did confess reams to Behrisch about the innkeeper's daughter and also celebrated her in numerous conventional ditties. In this light it is interesting to compare the Leipzig infatuation with the results of a love affair during his stay in Strasbourg, because he was almost totally silent about his affection for Friederike Brion, a country pastor's daughter in Alsace. We learn nothing of her from his letters to friends. There are a few of his own notes to her in a surprisingly calm and mature tone which would never let us suspect the volatility of his first original lyrics. These songs to Friederike are the most convincing in the German language until then, and perhaps for all time. Goethe's personality had by no means become a more stable mixture after he turned twenty. He had become more accustomed to its contradictions and its schizoid potential, even coming to believe that an individual has to have a mixed character to survive. With this acceptance of himself he was learning how to maintain a still delicate balance, and his first genuinely creative writing was associated with this effort. He was developing a wonderful competence in finding extremely satisfying forms even for his strongest feelings and harshest conflicts. The songs to Friederike constituted one of his first assurances in this regard.

His writing amounted to an independent personal discovery which bore out the theoretical speculations arrived at in discussions and debates with Herder. The genius, they argued, produces art spontaneously. Goethe was convinced that he wrote because he had to. He liked to use crass metaphors to get across the genuineness and immediacy of his need, letting an artist say, for example,

> That I with divine sense
> And human hand
> Know how to create,
> The same as with my woman
> I can, and like an animal must.[10]

When a friend asked him to make a particular literary contribution, he observed that it was a curious request "that I should write without the feeling, that I should give milk without having given birth."[11] Creativity understood as virtually instinctive response to an individual need became the mark of genius. The genius's work for that reason stands entirely alone and unique, not subject to any external rules whatever. The architect of the Strasbourg Cathedral "distinguishes himself mainly in the independence of his work, in that he, with no heed to what others have done, appears to have lived with his calling since the beginning of time."[12]

This concept of the *Originalgenie* was limited to Goethe's youth, yet the trait in his own personality, the need to create in order to maintain emotional stability, was permanent. He put it very simply to Charlotte: "When I lack a flow of new ideas to work on, I get sick."[13] The astute and sympathetic Schiller commented to Goethe years later: "It is just so, that nature determined you to be productive; any other condition, if it lasts for any length of time, conflicts with your being."[14] Such remarks as these strike to the heart of the matter. The boy had remained in a pathological state until he found remedy in his sketching and poetry. The first few years in which he recognized and proved their effectiveness, those in Strasbourg and Frankfurt, were characterized by the exuberance of the discovery.

He tried to live like a somnambulist, guided by an inner urge which could be felt most distinctly when his conscious intellect was numbed by daydream. Those who met him not only marked this quality, but often discussed it in a manner which betrays the influence of Goethe's own theorizing about it. Kestner in that description quoted earlier: "He follows the impulse of the instant and does not trouble himself with the consequences. This flows from his entire character, which is entirely original."[15] Goethe was convinced that a genius had to act in this way, and he turned his own poetic interests to precisely such personalities as his own. In the years that produced *Götz* and *Egmont* there were a host of other geniuses on his mind as well. He planned a Socrates drama; we have fragments of a Julius Caesar and a Mohammed. He progressed somewhat farther with a treatment of that archetype of creative man, resolute Prometheus, who, in defiance of the gods, shapes children with his own hands and gives them life.

He often spoke of his own literary works as his "children," and many of them were born in pain. This is especially true of *Faust* as it began to emerge in 1772-73, partly because it constituted a creative medium for the early frustrations already discussed: the boy's disappointment with learning and the promise of knowledge, his nervous exhaustion in a real or imagined love affair, and the sweet but thin hope of divine grace. The Faust-Mephistopheles personality had been shaped by those difficult experiences which distorted Goethe's own personality to an extent which he never fully overcame. This is probably why he had such great difficulty approaching the work again in Italy and why what he did add to it there, "Witch's Kitchen," is filled both with repugnant dream images and with phrases which the poet himself did not comprehend.

In those early, highly productive years he compared himself with Saint Sebastian, "bound to my tree, the arrows in my nerves, praising and glorifying God."[16] It is an interesting metaphor, in that it assumes suffering and the expression of suffering to be the whole point of his existence and as such, satisfying. He wrote a drama based on the *Memoirs* of Beaumarchais, and described the process to a friend:

> The beginning and end of all writing is the reproduction of the world around me by means of an inner world that seizes, combines, re-creates, kneads everything and gives it back again in its own appropriate form and style. That's the eternal secret, thank God, which I will not reveal to the gawkers and gossips. . . . That the *Memoirs* of that French adventurer Beaumarchais appealed to me and awakened in me the youthful power of romance, so that his character and his act amalgamated themselves with characters and actions in me, and my *Clavigo* emerged — that was good, for I took pleasure in it. What is more, I challenge the critic's knife to dissect the merely translated passages from the whole without mutilating it, without dealing a mortal wound not only to the plot, but to the structure, the living organism. But why talk about my children after they are born. They will make their own way under the broad heaven.[17]

The two last years in Frankfurt, the most productive ones Goethe ever experienced, were also restless years when he spent many hours on long hikes. There were more fragmentary projects than the large number which survive. They testify to an urge to create, unrelated to any thought of publication. Lyrics occurred to him more or less spontaneously (this was the period when he reported scrambling out of bed to get them on paper before they left him). Walking through the farm country south of Frankfurt he composed hymns as he went along. We have a half-incoherent dithyramb of gratitude chanted by the wanderer caught in a thundershower, wet but confident that the god of the rain is his kinsman. This is a thought which Goethe hesitated to express directly because it seemed so pagan and blasphemous, but was not his productive spirit godlike? Is not the genius a god wandering for a time on earth? It is amusing that he never made the fairly obvious connection between this idea and the Christian concept of the soul as pilgrim in a foreign land. Instead, he developed a symbolic view of himself as restless Wanderer-God, and he retained it for many years. It permitted him to overcome the sense of being whipped onward, Orestes-like, by ununderstood fears and passions. He could feel, rather, that his precipitate career was being guided by kindred "heavenly ones" toward some life's work which had "existed since the beginning of time." Compelled forward by *das liebe Ding,* a "sweet something" or inner urge, he could scorn mundane worries and with a bunch of field flowers in his hat stride full of self-awareness toward thunderheads on the horizon.

The penchant for hiking, which caused friends in the environs of Frankfurt to call him the Wanderer, was carried over to the Weimar life. Here his willingness to spend days at a time threading country lanes and labyrinthine forest tracks contributed significantly to the administration of the duchy. His restlessness now was greatly tempered by a sense of usefulness. We have to think of him on horseback, of course, and no longer on foot. The poetic reveries of these hours take the form of intimate personal discussions with the Lady Charlotte. They often rise to startling heights so that he can sometimes still capture them in a letter to her in the evening, or in a lyric. Both *Iphigenia* and *Tasso* took their beginnings on official trips during the especially fertile years 1779-80. Since he kept a diary from the time of his arrival in Weimar, we are able to calculate what a really remarkable amount of time he spent traveling, innumerable short trips being supplemented by frequent longer excursions. This side of his life can best be illuminated by reference to an excursion in the winter of 1777.

He was by this time convinced that he had found a satisfactory object for his restless energies in the public affairs of Weimar. He still flew from exuberance to despair, but he was sincere when he assured his friends that he was the happiest individual of all those he knew. He was on good terms with his sovereign, and the relationship with the Lady Charlotte had begun to take on its rare and lovely character. He felt at home in his cottage, "my little nest, soon now wrapped in storm, drifted over with snow."[18] He valued solitude, taking a deep pleasure in the "pure" frame of mind he could sometimes achieve when giving himself over entirely to communion with himself or with the absent beloved about immediate impressions and about ultimate destiny. The full-moon nights toward the middle of November drew him out of his cottage and elicited plans for a "secret trip" before the moon should wax full again. It was a foolhardy plan, to set out northward into the mountains alone at this time of year, but he had come to set particular store by giving remarkable undertakings the appearance of sane and sensible ones. The mining operations in Ilmenau justified an interest in the Harz region and could even be said to require a visit there. He had a much more personal motive, but he did not yet confide it even to his diary, partly because it was difficult, perhaps impossible, to articulate it; partly because he was afraid of breaking some kind of spell if he did.

Toward the end of the month the court set out for Eisenach on a hunting expedition, but Goethe had permission to make a "little detour." He gave no indication as to where it would take him. The letters he wrote along the way were mailed without place names. He set out at seven in the morning in a hard sleet and made twenty miles by noon, another five or six before dark. The next morning he was on his way by six again. "A hard freeze, and the sun came up in magnificent colors. I saw the Etter, the Insel and the Thuringian Mountains behind me. Then into the forest and, coming out, Sondershausen, very nicely situated. The peak of the Brocken momentarily glimpsed."[19] The Brocken is the highest peak in the Harz Mountains. Surrounded in legend of witchcraft, it was to become famous as the scene for the (as yet unwritten) Witch's Sabbath, or *Walpurgisnacht,* in *Faust.* To Goethe now, it was the goal of his journey.

"Night came soft and sorrowful. To Sachswerfen, where I had to take a guide with a lantern to get here [Ilfeld] through deep darkness. Found no room vacant. I am sitting in a little chamber beside the dining hall. Spent the entire day in constant purity."[20] His little room was normally the innkeeper's own, and Goethe delighted in using his peephole to observe the diners and drinkers. He was here under the name of Weber, an artist from Gotha. *Weben* (German for *to weave*) was one of his favorite poetic words, and he used it in many metaphorical contexts. Like the shuttle, he too was now being moved hither and yon, guided creatively by an unknown hand over a pattern in the forming.

For the moment, Weber's movements appeared quite deliberate.[21] His route was taking him straight north across to the other side of the Harz to Wernigeroda. Here he announced upon arrival at the inn that he would like very much to meet any "young persons who were known for scholarship and learning." There being only one such individual in the village, the superintendent's son, Carl Lebrecht Plessing, Weber was announced at the Plessing house and promptly invited for the evening. The young man was exactly Goethe's age. He felt that he had everything in common with Werther and had several months earlier written a letter (or rather a lengthy treatise) on his distraught state of mind to the author of *Werther,* but had waited in vain for a reply. Weber, coming from the region of Weimar, was naturally urged to speak about Goethe, and at last had to listen to the letter which Plessing had sent him (Plessing had retained a copy), and even to offer a conjectural explanation for Goethe's failure to answer. Plessing was a neurotic of an introspective sort, suffering from mild depression and encouraged in it by the sentimentality of the times. Goethe had come here in the hope that he might help him, but also with the dark feeling that here might be an *alter ego* who had somehow failed to come upon a path of stability and clarity. A kind of psychotherapy was indeed attempted that night in Wernigeroda, in that the artist Weber urged Plessing to open his eyes to his natural surroundings, to seek an objective grasp of them and use them as a creative outlet for his discontent. Weber claimed he had heard Goethe say, "We only save and free ourselves from a painful, self-reproaching and depressed state of mind by contemplation of Nature and whole-hearted participation in the objective world." For his own part, Weber could testify that he had experienced this truth as landscape painter, and he began to cite specific examples from the local countryside. Plessing interrupted him to declare that the objective world never lived up to his expectations. He had imagined these same things, he said, as looking quite different. This so alienated his guest that he left without revealing his identity, proceeding the next morning on to Goslar without calling again.

Goethe's route cannot even approximately be followed today, for it would take us through mine fields, over barbed wire, and past machine-gun towers, but the still feudal territorial boundaries of the eighteenth century permitted freedom of movement, so that Goethe simply skirted the northern edge of the Harz, albeit in "snow, sleet, and rain." He wrote to Charlotte:

I am drying my things now. They are hanging on the stove. How *little* man needs, and how sweet the recognition is of how much he needs this *little*. If you give me a present in the future, let it be something I can use on a trip like this. The mere piece of paper that the Zwieback was wrapped in, how many things I have used it for! I know that you will laugh and say that it finally went the way of all paper — but it is so. Your watch was a lovely bequest. I don't know now how this wandering trip will end, I am so accustomed to let myself be guided by destiny that I don't feel any urgency at all any more. Sometimes soft dreams of care glimmer through, but they will disappear again.

Good morning by candlelight. It is raining terribly, and no one travels except those in emergencies and on urgent business, and I, driven around in the world by strange ideas.

It is a peculiar sensation for me to move about in the world unknown. I think that I feel my relationship to people and things far more accurately. My name is Weber. I am a painter and have studied law. Or I am just a traveler, very polite to everyone and well received everywhere. Women have not concerned me. A pure calm and assurance surrounds me and, so far, everything has turned out well. The skies are clearing, we'll have a hard freeze tonight. It is first quarter. I have a wish for the full moon which, if the gods grant it, will require great thanks.[22]

He spent the next few days visiting mines to the south of Goslar.

I don't want to ask, and I don't want anyone else to ask what the restlessness is that lodges in me. When I am alone this way, I recognize myself again, just as I was in my early youth when I drifted through the world so entirely alone. People make the same sort of impression on me. Today, however, I found something out. As long as I was under pressure, as long as no one appreciated what was in me and developing in me, but — as is usually the case — either did not notice me at all or looked askance at me on account of a few of my rebellious idiosyncrasies, I did have a lot of wrong-headed, unbalanced notions, despite my good intentions. I can't explain it without going into specific instances. I was wretched, sick, oppressed, mutilated, call it what you will. . . .

I think of the duke a hundred times each day and wish him the enjoyment of a life like this, but he can't really savor it, he enjoys turning routine things into adventures too much to take real pleasure in treating the extraordinary as if it were routine.

It is just at that time of year, give or take a few days, when nine years ago I was at death's door and my mother, in deep distress, opened her Bible and found the verse, as she told me later: Thou shalt yet plant vines upon the mountains of Samaria; the planters shall plant and go forth in the dances of them that make merry. She found consolation for the moment, and has since taken great pleasure in the verse.[23]

She was, in fact, a great believer in Bible prophecy, and had "found" the verse by leafing through the Bible with her eyes shut and laying a needle on it.[24] Goethe was himself inclined to such superstitions. The moon was now full again, and he attached some kind of undefined prophetic significance to whether the skies would be clear and his unspoken wish fulfilled, to ascend the Brocken. He made the attempt on December 10 and seemed to regard it as one of the most important junctures in his life. Further excerpts from his record for Charlotte:

> The 10th before daylight. Before I leave here again, a good morning.
>
> In the evening just before seven. How shall I speak of the Lord with a goosequill, what song shall I sing of him? Now, when all my prose turns poetry and all poetry turns prose? It is not even possible for the lips to speak my fortune, how shall I evoke it with this pointed tool? — Dear Lady. God deals with me as with his prophets of old, and I know not whence it comes. When I ask for a sign, that the fleece be dry and upon all the ground there be dew, it is so. And the converse as well.[25] And, above all else, the more than motherly guidance of my wishes. The object of my desire has been attained, it hangs upon many threads, and many threads lead from it — the symbolic nature of my existence, which you know, and the humility which the gods are pleased to exalt, and the devotion which I observe at each and every moment, and the most complete fulfillment of my hopes.
>
> I will reveal to you (tell it to no one) that my journey was into the Harz, that my wish was to climb the Brocken, and now, dearest, I was up there today — in a quite routine manner, al-

though for the last week everyone has assured me that it was impossible. But how it all came about, and why, shall be postponed until I see you again — I will not even tell you now how eager I am.

I said I had a wish on the full moon. Now, dearest, I step out the door, and there stands the Brocken before me, high in the glorious moonlight above the spruces. And I was up there today, and made the dearest sacrifice of gratitude to my God on the Devil's Altar. . . .[26]

Only a word or two to serve as reminders. When I . . . came to the Peat House the Woods Keeper was sitting at his morning cup in his shirtsleeves. Our conversation touched on the Brocken, and he confirmed the impossibility of an ascension, told how often he had been up there in the summer and how foolhardy it would be to try it now. The mountains were concealed by the fog, and he said it would be that way up on top, too, that one could not see three paces ahead, and that anyone who did not know his way precisely, etc. There I sat with heavy heart, my mind half-occupied with the road back. I felt like the king whom the prophet commanded to smite upon the ground with the bow, but who did not smite enough times.[27] I silently prayed that the gods might turn the heart of this man — and the weather, too — but I said nothing. And he said to me: Now you can see the Brocken. I stepped to the window, and it was there before me as clear as my face in the mirror. My heart rose up, and I cried out: And should I not go up there? Have you no servant, no one? And he said: I will go with you.

I cut a sign in the window as testimony to my tears of joy, and if it were not to you I would think it a sin to tell about it at all. I did not believe it myself until the uppermost ridge. All the fog lay below, and above there was glorious clarity. All through the night until morning it was visible, also in the early daylight when I left.

The Brocken had provided one of those rare experiences which Goethe characterized as "the strange feeling of past and future in one," an assurance that the personality, although it may seem to have its existence in the moment only, does somehow partake of continuance in time. We would probably err if we tried to assign any more specific content to the sign which he read in the event of December 10, 1777. Like his mother's Bible prophecy, the successful Brocken ascent seemed to promise that the hidden powers guiding individual destiny were favorable, "motherly" disposed, and that in the end there would be rejoicing. It is very doubtful that he felt he had been promised success as a painter or as an author; indeed, the "dearest sacrifice" on the Devil's altar may have been just such artistic aspirations. These were the years when he still entertained ambitions in the political sphere. His practical justification for the Harz journey had been concern for the Weimar treasury. Like Faust, his aspirations were for the welfare of the land and its people. His Berlin visit occurred in the following spring; in the summer came the two major commissions, War and Roads. Now began those years of his life characterized by devotion to duty.

It is not a paradox that his most delicately inspired and formed dramas, *Egmont, Iphigenia,* and *Tasso,* occupied him in the midst of such work, because he found the one undertaking no less creative than the other. His diary of July 14, 1779:

God grant that field and meadow thrive, and that I get the feeling for this most fundamental of human efforts. Thoughts about the feeling for any occupation. Every work undertaken by man has what I would call a smell. Just as, on the tangible plane, the rider smells like horses, the bookstore of gentle mould, and the hunter's sphere like dogs, it is the same in nobler things. The material whence the forms are taken, the tools which one uses, the parts of the body which one exerts — all these things together lend the artist a certain domesticity and matrimony with his instrument. This intimacy with all the chords of the harp, the authority and assurance with which he touches them, will reveal the master in every art. He knows exactly what to look for . . . and does not daydream, the way I used to do in my drawing. When action is required, he does what is called for. Farming is especially attractive because it responds so clearly when I do something stupid or something right, and success or failure here is so fundamental to humanity. But I see in advance that it is not for me. I must not deviate from my prescribed path. My existence is just not a simple one. I only hope that I can gradually drain off all my presumptuousness and retain the noble ability to fill my true vessels to an equal height, one beside the other. We envy every man whom we see charmed to his potter's wheel; beneath his hands now a pitcher, now a bowl arises, in accordance with his will. To find the point where the manifold converges will ever remain a mystery, because the individuality of each of us must seek its own solution, and can listen to the advice of no one.

Since all efforts in Weimar depended on the duke's favor and on Goethe's ability to persuade him from one specific case to the next, however petty, the personal development of Carl August — twenty-one at the time of the diary entry just quoted — naturally remained Goethe's major concern. We are amused to read the remark, occasioned by an amateur performance of *Iphigenia* in the summer of 1779, that Carl August makes a good Pylades, "is trying hard, and gains almost daily in inner strength, composure, endurance, comprehension, and resolve."[28] Still, Goethe admits efforts to prevent his taking independent actions, especially in dealing with outsiders.[29] He is by no means satisfied with the young man's maturity, although he still entertains high hopes for his development.

In early August he wrote to his mother that he planned to come home for the first time in four years, reminding her that the vineyards on the mountains of Samaria had thrived and that there would be dancing besides.[30] Carl August was coming along; hence considerable preparations needed to be made. Goethe explained in detail the number of rooms and beds required for the group, but he cautioned that the duke "sleeps on a clean sack of straw," and requested the same for himself. He showed great concern for the simplicity of the arrangements, even at the risk of wounding his mother. "Get rid of all the candelabras in the duke's rooms. He would find them ridiculous."[31] There was no declared purpose for the trip. The Rhein-Main region was given out as the destination, but Goethe and Carl August had probably agreed to continue on into the Swiss Alps if circumstance and weather seemed favorably disposed. There is little doubt that Goethe was thinking of an educational journey in a sense closely related to his own trip to the Harz.

A party of five, Carl August and a chamberlain with one servant, Goethe and his man Seidel — the excellent secretary to whom we owe the complete records of this journey — arrived in Frankfurt in mid-September. After only a few days they took horses and rode down to Heidelberg, cutting west from there to the Rhine. Waiting for the ferry opposite Speier, Goethe wrote to Charlotte and made a first allusion to their destination. The weather was beautiful, he said, and they had decided "to drift around in the grand structures of this world and to bathe our spirits in the noble things of nature." He planned on this trip to "recapitulate my entire life up until now and see all my old friends again. God knows what the sum total will be."[32]

The main party continued down the river to a spot just north of Strasbourg which Goethe appointed — he was familiar enough with the region — while he made a little detour to Sesenheim, finding the parson's family little changed from eight years before. Even at our remove Friederike makes an extremely touching figure. In his autobiography Goethe recalled that her blond braids had been much too big for her delicate head. Frail and probably suffering from tuberculosis, she seems to have been an unusually attractive and good-natured child who had only ill-starred affairs with men. We have a credible report that she bore a child in later years, but she never married. The lovely story which Goethe tells about the Sesenheim romance in his autobiography was not written until after her death (at sixty-one). Even at that late date he recalled the oppressive guilt feelings that had accompanied him when he left her in 1771. He concludes his account in a curious way: "I extended my hand to her from my horse; tears stood in her eyes and I had a heavy heart. Then I rode down the path toward Drusenheim, and here a most remarkable vision came upon me. I saw, not with the eyes of the flesh but with those of the spirit, myself riding toward me along the same path in clothes such as I had never worn: pike gray trimmed in gold. I shook the dream off, and the figure disappeared. Nevertheless, it is remarkable that eight years later, in the livery as I had dreamed it, and which I was wearing not by intent but just by chance, I did find myself upon the same path, visiting Friederike once again."[33] There will be those who doubt such a vision. Let them regard it as Goethe's way of expressing a poetic confidence in the possibility of reconciliation.

Here is part of his contemporary account to Charlotte:

The younger daughter here had once loved me more than I deserved, and better than others on whom I have spent much passion and good faith. I had to forsake her at a moment when it almost cost her her life. She only touched lightly on what traces of the old illness remain, behaved most sweetly and with such cordial friendship from the first moment, when I surprised her on the threshold and we bumped noses, that I felt entirely at home. To her credit, I have to say that she did not seek to awaken the old feelings in my heart by the slightest allusion. She took me to every arbor, I had to sit there, and that was fine. . . . I found old songs I had written, a coach that I had decorated, we recalled tricks we had played in those good times, and I found their memory of me just as vivid as if I had not been away six months. . . . I stayed all night and left the next morning at sunrise, taking my departure from kind faces, so that I

am able again now to think of this corner of the world in satisfaction and live for myself in peace with these reconciled
spirits.[34]

This September brought a real harvest of reconciliation. Lili's
circumstances were the best imaginable, married to a wealthy
Strasbourg merchant with a *von* in his name. When Goethe
called on her, she proudly displayed her seven-week-old baby.
With Carl August and the rest of the party he continued on to
Emmendingen, visited the grave of his sister and called on her
widower with his new wife. The household seemed like a "tablet
where a beloved figure has been washed away."[35] From this point
on Goethe turned his entire concern to Carl August and the effects of the trip on him.

He recalled from his own first visit to the Alps a soul-expand-
ing sense of grandeur, and he hoped for a similar effect on the
younger man. More important, however, was the motto which he
had developed on his trip to the Harz: accomplishment of the
exceptional feat in a sure, matter-of-fact way. However, his old
dissatisfaction with Carl August seemed at first only to be aggra-
vated by the duke's foolish desire in the high mountains "to lard
the bacon, and with great effort and danger to seek just one more
purposeless, needless promontory."[36] This remark is from their
first excursion into the high Alps, south of Bern, and Goethe still
had hopes.

They returned to Bern, proceeded from there to Lausanne and,
after a loop north to the Lac de Joux, back down around
to Geneva. From here Goethe planned a daredevil route. First
they would visit the Savoy glaciers, then across into the Valise.
He was delighted to shock the Genevans "on their sofas and in
their cabriolets" by discussing the daring route with them, and
he liked to express his confidence that "if it is possible to ascend
the Brocken in December then these gates of terror must still let
us through in November."[37] Beyond the "gates of terror" lay yet

further difficulties and, Goethe hoped, an important lesson for his lord: how to undertake something quite out of the ordinary in cautious, competent safety. The chamberlain and his servant, even Philipp Seidel, took the easy route around the lake from Geneva to Lucerne. Goethe and the duke took a guide and crossed the Col de Balme between Chamonix and Martinique on November 6, hiked up the Rhone River and passed through the Furka in deep snow on the twelfth.

It was not as rash an undertaking as it appeared to be, but a well-considered decision made only after Goethe had sought the advice of no less an authority than the Geneva naturalist Horace Benoit de Saussure, whose judgment he supplemented with that of mountaineers at every important juncture along the way. Nevertheless, nervousness is clearly apparent from Goethe's diary, and the anxiety becomes more pronounced the closer they come to the Furka. The decision to visit Switzerland had been discussed with none in Weimar, and he would certainly be held responsible for any mishaps. The safety of a prince was in his hands. He by no means planned to persist in a dangerous crossing, but on the one hand there were imponderables to reckon with, and on the other hand, if the November snows were unexpectedly heavy, the whole point would be lost on Carl August. The extraordinary feat would either have to be undertaken at an unacceptable risk, or given up.

From Goethe's point of view a fundamental political lesson was involved. Leadership lay for him in the creative challenges it contained. A prince needed the originality to perceive necessary action, the patience to make a sure calculation, the courageous resolve to go ahead, and perseverance despite both difficulty and the protests of the philistines. Goethe would never be content for his prince, like so many of the nobility whom he had observed, to seek pleasure and excitement in the routine perquisites of sovereignty. The excitingly unexpected and unprecedented could be realized. What boggled petty minds like those of the timid Genevans when told of a November crossing of the Alps, could be accomplished by sure mastery of administrative routine — or so Goethe hoped in 1779. That he felt his pedagogical mission successful is indicated by his ordering a monument to be set up in Weimar commemorating the Swiss journey.

In these years the challenge of Weimar was absorbing much of Goethe's tremendous creative drive. Soon enough there came a period in which the frustrations of office seemed unbearable. The great, unanswered question was, of course, whether any substitute could be found for the steadying effect of administrative responsibility and tangible results for his energies.

NOTES

1. To Carl August on February 16, 1788.
2. *Italienische Reise,* March 1, 1788.
3. To Marianne Willemer on January 3, 1828.
4. August 7, 1779.
5. To Cornelia on October 18, 1766.
6. To Behrisch on November 7, 1767.
7. November 10-14, 1767.
8. To Behrisch in March, 1768.
9. To Langer on November 24, 1768. *DjG* 1, 260.
10. "Kenner und Künstler" (1774). *JA* 2, 103.
11. To Lavater in November, 1774.
12. To Roederer on September 21, 1771. *DjG* 2, 62.
13. December 28, 1782.
14. March 5, 1799.
15. To Hennings on November 18, 1772.
16. To Sophie de la Roche on September 15, 1774.
17. To Jakobi on August 21, 1774.
18. Diary, October 8, 1777.
19. Diary, November 30, 1777.
20. Ibid.
21. The following account is according to Goethe's *Campagne in Frankreich. JA* 28, 172 ff.
22. To Charlotte on December 4-6, 1777.
23. To Charlotte on December 9, 1777.

24. The reference is to Jeremiah 31:5, which Goethe misquotes slightly by mixing it with 31:4.
25. Allusion to Judges 6:38.
26. We can only speculate as to the nature of his "sacrifice," if indeed it was anything more than a gift of thanks. The Devil's Altar is a rock formation on the Brocken.
27. Allusion to II Kings 13:19.
28. Diary, early July.
29. Diary, July 30, 1779.
30. August 9, 1779.
31. Mid-August, 1779.
32. September 24, 1779.
33. *JA* 24, 64.
34. September 28, 1779.
35. To Charlotte on September 28, 1779.
36. Diary for Charlotte, October 14, 1779.
37. To Charlotte on November 2, 1779.

An Artist's Life

GOETHE was fond of observing that a work tends to be classified in accordance with the way it turns out. The journey to Switzerland was called a great success, the lords and ladies of Weimar expressing their admiration for the duke's exploits and how much the trip had done for him. Altruistic efforts seemed again to have improved Goethe's own situation, but little else. Switzerland firmly sealed a comradeship with Carl August that continued into their old age in good nature and mutual tolerance. Yet it is in the first months after their return from Switzerland that Goethe's impatience with his friend's qualifications for rule first becomes apparent, and letters to Charlotte show the results of their educational tour to have been less than completely satisfying. His assessment of the larger picture is revealed when he compares the tutors of young princes to "men entrusted with the course of a brook through a glen. They are charged with peace and quiet within that limited space, so they throw up a dam and store the water in a pretty pond. When the boy reaches maturity, the dam breaks and the water pours through, carrying violence and destruction, rocks and mud along with it. You marvel at what a great river this must be, until at last the supply dwindles and it becomes a brook again, as big or as little, as clear or as dull as nature made it, gurgling along its quite ordinary bed."[1]

Chafing under his own limited effectiveness, Goethe thought of himself as a bird caught up in yarn: "I know I have wings, but I cannot use them. Things will get better, however, and in the meantime I seek relaxation in history or dabble with a drama [*Tasso*], or a novel." Like many other diary entries, this one, from the end of April, 1780, continues into reflections about Carl August's prospects of improvement. Everything had appeared to depend on him; now Goethe was gradually resigning himself to doing the best he could on his own, seeking but not always obtaining the interest and accord of his prince. We have observed how his responsibilities increased until, by 1782, he had become the central governmental figure. He recognized that his own inner restlessness needed such tasks: "It is a need in my nature that compels me to undertake a variety of projects, and in the smallest village or on a desert island I would have to keep just this busy in order to survive."[2]

When he depreciated his writing as being something like a king's flute practice in idle hours,[3] it meant that his ministerial duties seemed to him to be the most challenging object available for his productive energy. They had certainly brought him at least a measure of the rewards and recognition which he craved, and precisely the active and effective role for which he longed in his early twenties, in the *Werther* days. His revisiting of Frankfurt, Sesenheim, and Strasbourg had left him with a sense of finally having got beyond those frustrated years, and in Geneva he declared: "When they ask me if I am not going to write something more [like *Werther*], I say, may God forbid that I am ever again in a condition to write thus."[4] Still, this "distant echo" among the public awakened his interest in writing, and he resolved to make better use of his talents in the future. Sure enough, he was scarcely back in Weimar before he recorded "a good idea, Tasso,"[5] a new work of precisely the same intimate confessional sort as *Werther*. He now read *Werther* for the first time since it had been in print. "I was astonished," he admitted to his diary.[6] For a man whose principal attention had turned to "order, precision, expedition" in public affairs,[7] whose free time went to cultivating his beloved garden on the Ilm and dabbling in light operettic diversions for the court, those old flights and plunges from rapture into despair seemed improbable indeed. He had not divorced himself entirely from poetry, but he had successfully "subordinated it to life"[8] — most of the time, at any rate. He admitted to Charlotte that there were occasions when, riding his official circuit, "the nag beneath me suddenly takes on a glorious form, an indomitable spirit, wings, and away she goes."[9]

Charlotte herself had been largely responsible for his subordination of poetry, even the poetry which she inspired, "to life." While in earlier years anxieties, frustrations, and guilt feelings had driven him to writing and drawing, calm and peace of mind were programmatic in the life of the soul as she conceived it for herself and Goethe. Their love reached its most idealized and most satisfying peak in these years just after 1780. The two began to use the familiar form of address in private, then even in their letters. She tacitly acknowledged her inclination to him, and at last openly granted the high favor of her love. Before Switzerland he had been attracted to her by a wish to understand and help — a wish not entirely free from vanity. Now his own need for her became the paramount, ever repeated theme of his letters. Here are some excerpts from the spring of 1781.

"On my knees I beg you, complete your work, make me truly good."[10]

"The candor and calm of my heart, which you have given back to me, shall be for you alone."[11]

"May your good spirit be ever with me, and may the presence of the dear law make me good and make me happy."[12]

"Receive me with your love, and help me across the dry soil

of clarity the same as you have accompanied me through the vale of mist."[13]

In just what the "dear law" consisted is not at all clear. Maintenance of inner calm through diligence and concern for others is a major motif in the letters to Charlotte. He assures her again and again that he is working on *Tasso* or on some other substantial project in order to earn his hours with her. Sometimes the "dear law" may strike us as a little trivial, as when he assures her on New Year's of 1782 that he is going to stay home and paint even though he does not want to, in order "right at the beginning to obtain a victory over myself." We are never certain just what the failings are which the Lady is helping him correct, but his characteristically abrupt changes in disposition may be the main issue. It was also in the spring of 1781 that he called "the element of which the human soul is formed and in which it lives a purging fire in which all the powers of heaven and hell are in motion and active."[14] Remaining ever in Charlotte's presence while they are apart steadies and smooths his moodiness, and their spiritual inseparability lends transcendental, even religious luster to their relationship. Charlotte was herself inclined to believe in the transmigration of souls, and Goethe asserted that in some other life she must have been his sister, or his wife. Objects which she gave him took on a sacramental character; he compared his confiding in her with confessions to a priest, and each spring he sent her "first fruits" from his garden.

Yet these things constitute only one segment in his extraordinarily broad range of metaphors — here are a few from the winter of 1780-81: "Tell me that you are well and that you will extend my term on the capital which I so much need in my far-flung and dangerous mercantile business."[15]

"I can send you no rhymes, for my prosaic life swallows these rivulets like broad sand, but the poesy of loving my best one cannot be taken from me."[16]

"I can only with difficulty refrain from gazing into my dearest mirror."[17]

"My heart is like a robber's castle that you have now occupied, driving the occupants out. Now value it enough to set a watch there. . . . Since I am the eternal simile maker I told myself yesterday that you are to me what an Imperial Commission is to the territorial prince. You teach my heart, which has run up debts everywhere, to be more economical, to take its happiness in pure income and outflow. The only difference is, my best one, that you, unlike all accounting commissions, allow me fuller competence over my holdings than I had before."[18]

"Your love surrounds me with a more and more healthful climate, so that through you I shall soon recover from my lingering sins and faults."[19]

"Your love is my morning and evening star, setting after the sun and arising before it."[20]

The drama fragment *Tasso* of 1780-81 was itself a more extended and perhaps more explicit metaphor for their love. The title figure is the Italian Renaissance poet whose *Jerusalem Delivered* was among the classics familiar to well-bred children like Wolfgang and Cornelia Goethe. A courtly poet, he counted among his patrons the Duke of Ferrara, to whose sister he was strongly attached. She was, however, unattainable for one of his estate. His own irritability and feelings of persecution led to a falling out with his patron, who placed him in a convent. He escaped and, disguised as a peasant, wandered on foot to his sister Cornelia in Sorrento, where he is said to have found peace and healing. He was, however, to spend much of the rest of his life in wandering, depression, and even harsh incarceration in the madhouse. Goethe seems to have perceived parallels between his own condition and Tasso's, and in the fall after he returned from Switzerland, he began trying to lend them a dramatic form. He kept adding to the piece for about a year, but came up with no real plot and seems never to have got beyond the second act. As it stood it was a kind of homage to his own unattainable lady. He reported his progress to her faithfully; when she at last returned his love, the *Tasso* fragment ceased to hold his interest.

From our point of view it constitutes a revealing projection of their relationship. In 1782 Goethe was himself ennobled, but until that time a social barrier comparable to that between Tasso and his princess also affected Goethe's life at court. The peripeteia of the drama occurs when Tasso, overstepping these feudal limits, seeks to embrace the princess and is banished from her presence as a consequence. This is a misfortune for both parties, for Tasso brought the only joy into her secluded existence, still never completely free of an illness into which his coming had cast the first hope. She has no interest in marriage, but looks forward to a serene life with Tasso and with her brother in Ferrara. The most famous passages in the finished drama are those in which the princess teaches Tasso not to long for the fabled golden age, and argues that if such ever existed it can still be realized in the conduct of the individual life. Against his vision of an era when society permitted whatever was enjoyable, she sets her famous dictum that the permissible is the seemly. How shall men know what beseems them? Let them ask, she says, a noble woman.

While the *Tasso* fragment was indeed faithfully autobiographical, it singled out only one strand of Goethe's personality, the poetic existence which he had found by itself to be entirely too precarious, even verging on insanity — as *Werther* could at any time remind him. Still, he somehow felt that this must be his true self, and we are amused to note how the Tasso fate, to wander alone and banished from those who once appreciated him, had long occupied his fancy. Scarcely installed in office in Weimar, he wrote to Charlotte in 1776 that the thought had pierced his soul: "When this, too, you must leave one day, the land where you have found so much . . . the wanderer's staff in your hand, just as you left your homeland. Tears came into my eyes, and I felt the strength to bear that fate, too."[21] Such imaginings strike us as a little childish, but we must at least admit that Goethe never deceived himself about the instability of his personality. As a very young man he made a remark typical of this astute self-awareness: "I am just like other good people, sane up to a point."[22] Although alarmed by his own problems, he recognized that any distinction between "sane" and "insane" would have to be a very tenuous one, and he intuitively looked to the one condition for clarification and understanding of the other.

The widespread institutionalization of the mentally ill, injured, and deteriorated is a modern, urban phenomenon. In the eighteenth century eccentrics were tolerated, hypochondriacs indulged, and the melancholy romanticized. Inhabitants of a city like Frankfurt were in general much more familiar with the deranged and feeble-minded than they are today. It is Goethe's special merit that he recognized many such cases as curable illnesses, and in several instances actually undertook treatments which cost him considerable effort and money. Unfortunately, no study of this aspect of his activity has been undertaken. Still, a rough survey of his experiences before Italy shows him occupied with an astonishingly large number of individuals whom we would regard as sufficiently neurotic to need psychiatric help: a good number of middle-aged and old depressives, several seriously neurotic cases, two of whom were suicides, as well as at least three genuine psychotics.[23] For this last group he was able to find little sympathy or understanding, perhaps sensing that there was nothing he could do for them. In any case, it was to milder cases of mental illness that he turned his attention and efforts. His autobiographical writings contain careful observations and competent descriptions of them; his letters and often even his poetry reveal numerous attempts to help them.

A study of this subject would probably concentrate first on his observations of the neurotics he remembered from childhood and youth.[24] Other main topics would be his abortive effort on behalf of Plessing, which we discussed in the previous chapter, and his more persistent treatment of Kraft, an unfortunate whom he supported in the years 1779-85. The letters to Kraft supply our best evidence of Goethe's therapeutic skill and his favorite technique of requesting objective accounts of his life and problems from the patient himself. It is obvious that the better-known poetic works are all based on a deep understanding for psychological difficulties, but a special study of this topic would also dwell on certain minor works which appear to have been written with specific psychotherapeutic ends in view, like the operettas written on the duchess's birthday. *Lila,* for example, deals with the treatment of a young woman who is gradually brought to recognize her husband, whom she has insisted must be dead.

Goethe's strong interest in mental illness and in its treatment was related to his own personality problems. He undertook continual self-diagnosis, and he recognized that the more extensive his observations of other cases were, the better he could appreciate his own. Werther, who develops pronounced paranoid symptoms just before his suicide, shows how well Goethe understood the transition from normal to abnormal states, and indeed at a very early age. It was in this youthful period that he confessed himself, like others, "sane up to a point." As the years passed, he tended more and more to analyze his own conflicts in terms of a polarity between artistic and practical demands. As early as 1780 he compared himself with a bird attempting to live underwater — "The fish are troubled about him and cannot understand why he does not go ahead and thrive in their element."[25] This was at the same time that he was claiming to have succeeded in subordinating his poetry to life.

The best period of his love for Charlotte corresponds, as we have seen, with the "bird's" most successful accommodation to the Weimar element. From 1782 we have Goethe's own rather objective account of the day-to-day compromise. "I have been living very happily for a time. I scarcely leave the house, but take care of my duties and in good hours write down the tales which I have always been used to telling myself." He has been going over his old works and has sent *Werther* "back into the womb" for revision. Papers and letters from the 1770's have been collected and bound, for he wants to be able to survey "as from a hilltop, the long valley through which I have wandered." He claims that he has developed various methods to separate his political and social life entirely from his poetic existence.

> Thus I begin to live for myself again. My dream that the sweet seeds germinating in my personality and in my friends can be planted only in this soil, or that such heavenly jewels could be set in the earthly crowns of these princes, has been given up entirely, and I find the happiness of my youth restored. Just as it never occurred to me in my father's house to combine juridical practice with the manifestations of my spirit, I now separate the Privy Councilor from my other self, and the Privy Councilor gets along very well. Only in the center of my plans, resolves, and projects do I remain secretly true to myself, thus tying my social, political, moral, and poetical life together in a hidden knot.[26]

The period's fortunate balance of his greatest devotion to Charlotte and busiest dedication to office was almost always difficult to maintain. Slipping away to the Harz in 1777 was one of various attempts at temporary retreat from mundane demands into a true self, conceived in essentially poetic terms. Since his writings offered him a refuge in a sense very similar to that of an actual physical retreat, the flight to Italy with its literary chores constituted the most significant of his poetic withdrawals from Weimar's practical demands. We have seen how, as the months passed in Rome, he came to speak of himself more and more openly and frequently as "nothing but an artist." Still, he probably at no time thought of Italy as more than a temporary escape from the harsh world of practicality and reality. Just as he planned to have the edition of his works finished by Easter, 1788, he also expected to be back in the stream of things in Weimar by about that time. It is revealing of his attitude that he felt pangs of conscience as soon as he started out for Italy, confessing that he was just giving in to his "childish nature," and resolving to make up for such self-indulgence when he got back.[27] Before Italy he clearly felt that the world of practical affairs had just claims upon him. Indeed, he had experienced peace of mind over extended periods only with the help of its demands.

The maturer, less excitable man was experiencing a gradual shift in ethical attitudes. In the very first months among the richer sensual offerings of Italy he was willing to think more in terms of his own continuing education and personal development, less and less in terms of his value and usefulness to others. It was a point of view in line with his growing conviction in theoretical biology that each and every organism must develop according to unique inner needs and hence cannot be judged by external criteria. In later years he liked to declare that "the purpose of life is life itself," and the firmness with which he came to maintain this view corresponds with the more subjective ethical stand assumed in Italy.

One of our first evidences of his new philosophy of life comes just at the time of settling down to a new lifestyle in Rome in the summer of 1787. He told Charlotte that he was becoming acquainted with people who impressed him with a kind of happiness that seemed to come from the harmony of their condition. "Even the lowliest, when he is entire, can be happy and, in his own way, perfect. That is what I want. I must get it, and I can, too. At least I know where it can be found, and I have become inexpressibly better acquainted with myself on this trip."[28] He has evolved a new self-centeredness which would have been unthinkable for that pre-Italian Goethe who so longed to be useful to others. He now wants only to make the most of one life, and claims to have found "that all really clever people, one way or another, realize and, whether with finesse or bluntly, insist that the moment is all important, so that the only advantage an intelligent man has consists in living in such a way that his life, insofar as he can control it, contains the largest possible concentration of intelligent, happy moments."[29] An extension of thinking along these lines led naturally back to art, where an opportunity seemed to present itself for relating infinitely more "intelligent, happy moments" to one's own limited existence. "My only interest has been in *producing,* ever since the time when I perceived how whatever you *produce,* even if it is not the most perfect, is reviewed — that is, it tells about our existence — for millennia."

Certain reports from Weimar could be interpreted as justification for giving more attention to his own well-being. Philipp Seidel, terrifically jealous of his absent master's position and prerogatives, fastened Weimar officialdom with a suspicious eye, promptly reporting to Rome first the inevitable misunderstandings about official commitments made by Goethe before he left, then in time the government's essential adjustments to his extended absence. News of the latter gave rise to mixed feelings. "Since I shared the whim of Charles V to witness my own funeral while still alive, I must not be surprised when the pallbearers and gravediggers do their work, and the priests intone the exequies."[30] Of course, it had been Goethe's own wish to give up some of his offices, or even all of them.[31] Still, his official capacity had in the past contributed greatly to his self-esteem, earned him the respect of others, and allowed Charlotte and Carl August to regard him as indispensable. For a century and a half now the world has taken Goethe to be a poet, so that from our remove it is not easy to appreciate the seriousness of his decision to give up his political position in that moribund establishment even though it had constituted his only way of life during his adult years.

The problematic nature of his new capacity — or lack of capacity — in Weimar may have contributed to Goethe's hesitation to leave Rome according to his original plans. He stayed and for ten months gave himself over to a life strikingly out of character with his hitherto disciplined and productive career. He became a dawdler in *osterias,* a painter, a dabbler in music, a crony and patron of artists, a carefree sightseer — it was as near to a bohemian existence as Goethe ever came. The Privy Councilor had not been his true self — didn't even, as he said, need his true self. During these Roman months he tested the assumption that the true self was an artist, and he tried to prepare his friends to receive him back to Weimar as such.

In early 1788 he read a new Tasso biography by Pierantonio Serassi (1785), the first scholarly treatment of that poet's life. He continued to feel an affinity for Tasso and to interpret Tasso's problems as metaphorhically his own. Hence he read about the poet's clash with a competent Ferrara minister, Antonio Montecatino, in the light of his own inner conflicts. His old *Tasso* fragment interested him again, and he began to rewrite it now with two central masculine figures: the poet juxtaposed with the man of affairs, Antonio Montecatino. While Tasso is fully aware of his own divine gift and hence imbued with a high sense of the poet's mission, he neverthless looks upon Antonio with pathological envy: success in the practical world earns not merely the esteem of their prince, the Duke of Ferrara, but (what is far more important) his confidence as well. Tasso is not blind to the advantages his duke derives from patronage of an artist like himself, and he knows that the duke values him on this account. But he feels thrust out into a less real world, where he longs desperately to be like Antonio, a genuine companion and collaborator with the duke.

Antonio has a high regard for poetry and is not free of envy himself, yet he cannot overcome his contempt for the willful, self-indulgent childishness of the poetic personality. His need for appreciation and recognition is no less strong than Tasso's, but while Tasso enjoys the solicitations of tender ladies at court, he must waste his hours and days in a cold world of intrigue and contention. Despite his aversion to Tasso, Antonio does, as a sane man, have some understanding for the poet's problems. Tasso, on the other hand, lost in introspection and illusions of persecution, hates Antonio.

In a last letter from Rome Goethe tells Carl August that he would not be working on *Tasso,* would not have chosen it; it is a part of his past which has chosen him. "Just as the impulse which led me to this subject arose from the depths of my nature, the effort which I must now expend to finish it forms a strangely appropriate end to my Italian career, and I would not wish it otherwise."[32] *Tasso* was the work which occupied his thoughts on his way north. He found it appropriate, while wandering, to go over in his mind "the fortunes of a man whose entire life was spent in wandering hither and yon."[33] During the first year back in Weimar progress on *Tasso* is mentioned at fairly regular intervals, and by the summer of 1789 he was sending it to the printer in installments. Both the final manuscript and the printer's proof were read with great care, the most attentive preparation recorded for any of his works. Such concern for minute detail indicates that Goethe had come to look upon *Tasso* as a particularly lucid facet of his own being. When he first began developing this character in the early 1780's, the embodiment of the extremely problematic artistic personality was envisioned as hanging on and steadied by the noble princess; the finished drama leaves Tasso dependent on the well-secured existence of Antonio and deprived of his princess's love. Thus the poet ends in mental anguish, no solution being offered.

That period in which *Tasso* was reworked was one of the most problematical ones in the mature Goethe's life. Since he had severed his old official ties in Weimar, readjustment would not have been easy in any case. In his uncertainty about the intended new role, a kind of poet in residence in Weimar, he wrote to Carl August from Rome: "Without the participation of those to whom destiny has firmly bound me, without their approval, I do not care to, nor am I able to take pleasure in anything. All notions of living without them are only phantoms of a delirium which goes away when the fever passes."[34] But he did in fact find himself isolated from all his friends when he returned to Weimar. Many were simply less interesting to him than before on account of their provinciality and priggishness. Carl August was absent on military exploits, Herder had gone off to Italy, and Goethe found himself adrift in an uneventful vacuum. He had long dreaded the possibility of living in Weimar without Herder — for example, when Herder had been offered a position at the University of Göttingen in 1786, he had told Charlotte, "Except for you and him I would be alone here."[35] Now, with Herder in fact gone, he felt that a "dismal sky had absorbed all the colors."[36]

Under the circumstances his vulnerability to the companionship of Christiane Vulpius is the more understandable, but of course the union with her tended to finalize estrangement from Weimar society as soon as it became known. It would not be right to look on her as the cause of the disease; she was only a complicating symptom. We have observed how Goethe had already alienated the Lady Charlotte even before he met Christiane, and long before Charlotte knew about her; we have also seen how Christiane even then seemed to Goethe to be no real obstacle to their continued friendship, but on the contrary an additional incentive for him to desire its renewal. Without Herder, without Charlotte, his dream of an artistic existence probably seemed absurd to him. He lacked all intellectual contact and stimulation. Without the prestige of high office, how was his life now to differ from that of a well-to-do philistine? For some time the only activities which elevated his existence were his scientific research and various well-intended efforts on behalf of Thuringian cultural life.

Weimar society and Weimar propriety are epitomized at their best in the Lady Charlotte von Stein. By taking note of Goethe's principal differences with her, we can better appreciate the impossibility of their further compatibility and thus illustrate his relationship with Weimar circles in general.

Most people do not change their ways very fundamentally at her age (she was now forty-six), but Goethe had changed radically since he had left her. He had become much more objective and matter-of-fact, even pragmatic, in his assessment of the world, himself, and his fellow man. Aversion to Roman Catholicism had provided him with a last thrust in the direction of a thoroughly secular attitude toward the lot of man, while Charlotte continued in that gentle sentimentality which had been fashionable when she and Goethe first met, allowing a devout Protestantism more and more to color her feelings about Providence and the human situation. She accepted conventional moral standards and applied them to others in the same way as she expected certain conventions in etiquette to be observed by those around her. She had taught Goethe all these things herself in his early years at court. Now he, on the other hand, was fully prepared to accept all of life just as he found it, unvarnished by Weimar propriety.

A major difference between the two now was in their radically different concepts of how a man should justify his existence, although it probably was never discussed between them. She still assumed that Goethe ought to devote himself to the duke as she did herself to the duchess, and through the sovereign couple to the general welfare of their fellow men. Although Goethe would in fact play a greater role in Weimar affairs in the years to come, just after his return he still cherished his Italian ideal of cultivating his individual existence in an artistically satisfying manner. Two good observers were his old friend Knebel and the interested stranger Friederich Schiller. Knebel: "Art has won him entirely. He regards it as the goal of all human betterment. I can comprehend this from his point of view, if I accept the flower of sensuality as the pinnacle of existence."[37] Schiller: "So far as I know, observe, and hear, Goethe has not been able to speak openly to anyone. His intellect and his myriad connections win him friends, admirers, and adulation, but he has continued to hold back and to keep to himself. I fear that he has made the utmost enjoyment of his own *amour propre* into an ideal of happiness which does not make him very happy."[38]

No break with Charlotte occurred. The old relationship with her simply could not be renewed. Although he appears to have been the more active party in trying to do so, he admitted later that he recognized it was he who had changed.[39] What was true of his old friendship with her applied generally to his previous Weimar existence. No significant points of contact could be found. Goethe had to begin a new life at forty, and his old associates could scarcely be expected to look on in full approval. One saw him seldom. He accompanied Carl August on shorter and on extended campaigns, to Silesia in 1790, Valmy in 1792, and Mainz in 1793. When at home he withdrew to his great townhouse and walled garden — he was jealous that no alien windows be permitted to overlook it — and here he followed a well-nourished middle-class existence with Christiane and their baby son (born on Charlotte's birthday in 1789). His visits to Jena were frequent because of his research projects, and they grew more extended after he became interested in Schiller in 1794. But Goethe had become a stranger to Weimar society not only because one saw him seldom; on the contrary, associations had ceased to exist because he had become a stranger to their ways. Charlotte wrote to Fritz in 1796 that she had encountered Goethe quite by chance in Jena: "A little winged victory arrived for him from Dresden while I was there. He set it on the table before him and said we can best discuss art while eating and drinking. In fact, he took no further interest in anyone there, and at last he had his glass of wine in one hand and the statuette in the other."[40]

NOTES

1. To Charlotte on April 11, 1782.
2. To Knebel on December 3, 1781.
3. To Kestner on May 14, 1780.
4. To Charlotte on November 2, 1779.
5. Diary, March 30, 1780.
6. April 30, 1780.
7. To Kestner on May 14, 1780.
8. Ibid.
9. September 14, 1780.
10. March 12, 1781.
11. March 27, 1781.
12. April 18, 1781.
13. May 3, 1781.
14. To Lavater on May 7, 1781.
15. December 16, 1780.
16. January 1, 1781.
17. January 8, 1781.
18. March 8, 1781.
19. March 19, 1781.
20. March 22, 1781.
21. July 16, 1776.
22. To the Kestners on September 15, 1773.

23. Cornelia and the Duchess Louise were mildly neurotic; Jerusalem and Merck, suicides. The amanuensis maintained by Goethe's father while Goethe was in Frankfurt, also the poet Reinhold Lenz (that friend from Strasbourg who followed Goethe to Weimar) and the Count von Lindau, the previous guardian of Peter im Baumgarten, would be classified by the modern clinician as psychotic.

24. Of close associates in Frankfurt, *Dichtung und Wahrheit* makes clear the neuroses of Goethe's teacher Thym, and of Count Thoranc, the French officer quartered with his family in the last years of the Seven Years War.

25. To Charlotte on September 14, 1780.

26. To Knebel on November 21, 1782.

27. Diary, September 6, 1786.

28. June 8, 1787.

29. *Italienische Reise*, October 27, 1787.

30. To Seidel on May 15, 1787.

31. To Carl August on May 27, 1787.

32. To Carl August on March 28, 1788.

33. To Bertuch on April 5, 1788.

34. February 3, 1787.

35. July 14, 1786.

36. To Charlotte on July 22, 1788.

37. Knebel to Herder on November 7, 1788. Herwig I, 452.

38. February 5, 1789. Herwig, 464.

39. E.g., Charlotte to Fritz on November 29, 1795. Herwig, 623.

40. Charlotte to Fritz on May 16, 1796. Herwig, 639.

Chronological Index

Topical Index

The notes are indexed for Goethe's works only.

Topical Index

Topical Index